Wilhelm Reiss, Alphons Stübel, Wilhelm Greve

The Necropolis of Ancon in Peru

Vol. 2

Wilhelm Reiss, Alphons Stübel, Wilhelm Greve

The Necropolis of Ancon in Peru
Vol. 2

ISBN/EAN: 9783337217334

Printed in Europe, USA, Canada, Australia, Japan

Cover: Foto ©ninafisch / pixelio.de

More available books at **www.hansebooks.com**

THE
NECROPOLIS OF ANCON
IN PERU

A CONTRIBUTION TO OUR KNOWLEDGE OF

THE CULTURE AND INDUSTRIES

OF THE

EMPIRE OF THE INCAS

BEING THE RESULTS OF EXCAVATIONS MADE ON THE SPOT

BY

W. REISS AND A. STÜBEL

TRANSLATED

BY

PROFESSOR A. H. KEANE, B. A. F. R. G. S.
VICE PRESIDENT OF THE ANTHROPOLOGICAL INSTITUTE

WITH THE AID OF THE GENERAL ADMINISTRATION OF THE ROYAL MUSEUMS OF BERLIN

SECOND VOLUME.

BERLIN

A. ASHER & Co.

1880—1887.

SOLE AGENTS FOR AMERICA DODD, MEAD & COMPANY NEW YORK, 755 BROADWAY

The Peruvian Indian costume consisted essentially of vest and smock-like upper garments, the former covering the upper part of the body only, the latter reaching half way down the thigh, and apparently often almost to the knee. Loin-girdles, loosely worn cloths, head-dress and foot-coverings completed the costume, which afforded scope for much ornamentation. Thus are the subjects of the Incas described by the Conquistadors and their successors, and thus are they exhibited in the paintings on the finer earthenware, of which an instructive example is given by the picture of a costume introduced into the third volume, Plate 101.

Head-dress and foot-coverings being reserved for the following section, here the garments proper alone will be treated, that is, those woven articles of attire, whose form enables us to receive how they were worn. Such are the Poncho-like garments, the robes of a Talaria type worn for elegance or distinction, and lastly cloths and loin-girdles.

All the Plates in this Division have been executed by Herr P. Schulz.

PLATES
OF THE
SECOND VOLUME

GARMENTS AND TEXTILES

(PLATES 35- 74a)

In the second volume, comprising Parts 5—7, are exhibited the native garments and textiles, products of an industry our knowledge of which has been conspicuously disclosed by the sepulchral finds at Ancon.

The garments and what fragments survive of them present, jointly with doll-like clay figures and the representations occurring on vases, a picture of the application of the woven materials so diversely and often so richly ornamented. Thus is afforded a clear idea of the garb and style of dress prevalent amongst the Indians of that period.

The greater part of the volume is devoted to a faithful reproduction of the textiles. The pieces figured in natural size, or at all events only on a slightly reduced scale, throw light on the local methods of weaving, and give at least an approximate notion of the effect of the richly-coloured designs.

A supplement to the garments is formed by the pouches, for which fabrics often peculiarly ornamented were specially woven.

SUMMARY

OF THE

PLATES OF THE SECOND VOLUME.

V. Garments . .   Plates 35–44
VI. Textiles   45—71
VII. Pouches   72. 74a

LIST OF PLATES

IN THE

SECOND VOLUME.

V. Garments.

a. Garments of the Poncho Type.

39.	Bright Woollen Garments	Plate 35
40.	Simple Woollen Garments	„ 36
41.	Garments of Wool and of Cotton with Woollen Patterns	„ 37
42.	Simple Cotton Garments	„ 38
43.	Painted Cotton Garment	„ 39
44.	Various kinds of Garments	„ 40

b. Garments of the Talaria Type.

45.	Materials for Robes of the Talaria Type	„ 41
46.	Large Robes of the Talaria Type	„ 42
47.	Ornamented Robes of the Talaria Type, with accompanying trimmings	„ 43

c. Cloths and Loin-cloths.

48.	Dress Materials	„ 43a
49.	Loin-Girdles and Woollen Cloths	„ 44

VI. Textiles.

a. Pieces of Woollen Garments.

50.	Gobelins fabric ornamented in superior style	„ 45
51.	Counterpart of Material on previous Plate	„ 46
52.	Half of a fine Woollen Garment	„ 47
53.	Richly ornamented Woollen Dress	„ 48
54.	Sumptuous Garment of a Mummy	„ 49
55.	Tapestry with figures of Warriors	„ 50
56.	Gobelins Materials with Human figures — Portions of Woollen Garments	„ 51
57.	Gobelins Fabrics with Human and Animal figures — Portions of Woollen Garments	„ 52
58.	Three Gobelins Pieces with Human figures — Portions of Woollen Garments	„ 53
59.	Figured Gobelins with Geometrical and Animal designs — Portions of Woollen Garments	„ 53a
60.	Dress Materials with Geometrical Patterns	„ 54
61.	Gobelins Stuffs with Geometrical Patterns and Animal figures — Parts of Woollen Garments	„ 55
62.	Dress Materials and Borderings	„ 55a
63.	Woollen Gobelins fabrics with Animal figures	„ 56

b. Cotton Stuffs ornamented with Wool.

64.	Boldly ornamented dress Materials	Plate 57
65.	Ornamental Cotton Garment with Woollen border	„ 58
66.	Dress Materials horizontally striped	„ 59
67.	Cotton dress Materials	„ 59a

c. Passementerie Work.

68.	Dress Materials with Passementerie trimmings	„ 60
69.	Passementerie Work	„ 60a

d. Trimmings for Robes of the Talaris Type.

70.	Border of a Robe of the Talaris Type	„ 61
71.	Woollen border of a flowing Garment	„ 62
72.	Trimmings of robes of the Talaris Type — Woollen Materials	„ 62a
73.	Borders of flowing Garments — Ornamented Woollen Corner pieces	„ 63

e. Corners and trimmings of simple Cotton fabrics and dresses.

74.	Ornamental Corners	„ 64
75.	Cotton Cloths with ornamental Corners and Hem	„ 64a
76.	Ornamental Hems of small Cotton cloths	„ 64b
77.	Woollen trimmings of Cotton garments	„ 65
78.	Cotton Materials with Woollen trimmings	„ 65a

f. Borderings.

79.	Broad Gobelins Woollen Borderings	„ 66
80.	Borders and border-like fabrics	„ 66a
81.	Borderings and Sleeve trimmings	„ 67
82.	Borderings of Garments	„ 67a
83.	Woollen Borders of Cotton garments	„ 67b
84.	Woollen Dress Borderings	„ 68
85.	Border-like Woollen fabrics	„ 68a
86.	Woollen Borders and Cotton dress Materials	„ 68b
87.	Woollen Borders	„ 69
88.	Pieces of insertion of Woollen Band	„ 69a
89.	Sundry pieces of weaving	„ 69b
90.	Diverse kinds of simple dress Materials	„ 69c

g. Loosely woven net-like Materials.

91.	Loosely woven and reticulated Stuffs	„ 70
92.	Loosely woven and reticulated Cotton stuffs	„ 70a
93.	Cotton stuffs reticulated and ornamented with Needlework	„ 71

VII. Pouches.

94.	Large and small girdle pouches	„ 72
95.	Woollen hanging bags	„ 73
96.	Woollen, Cotton and Net pouches	„ 74
97.	Pouch Materials	„ 74a

V.
GARMENTS.

(PLATES 35—44.)

PLATES OF PART V.

a. Garments of the Poncho Type.

39. Bright Woollen Garments	Plate	35
40. Simple Woollen Garments	„	36
41. Garments of Wool and of Cotton with Woollen Patterns	„	37
42. Simple Cotton Garments	„	38
43. Painted Cotton Garment	„	39
44. Various kinds of Garments	„	40

b. Garments of the Talaria Type.

45. Materials for Robes of the Talaria Type	„	41
46. Large Robes of the Talaria Type	„	42
47. Ornamented Robes of the Talaria Type, with accompanying trimmings	„	43

c. Cloths and Loin-cloths.

48. Dress Materials	„	43a
49. Loin-Girdles and Woollen Cloths	„	44

PLATE 35.

BRIGHT WOOLLEN GARMENTS.

(⅐ of the natural size.)

Although woven tissues and dress materials were found in all the graves, complete and fully preserved garments are comparatively rare. The most frequently recurring garment corresponds to the Poncho still common in South America; but, as already mentioned, both sides are sewed together in such a way as to leave no opening except for the arms. These articles of attire were mostly composed of two parts so arranged, that the slit for the head coincides with the seam. Many are so broad across the shoulders that when worn the arms were covered down to the hands. Hence when using the arms the dress had apparently to be gathered up in numerous folds on the shoulders.

Fig. 1. An almost square garment of a somewhat coarse but very thick and strong material. Each colour being woven separately is divided from the neighbouring colours by small spaces running with the warp. Wider gaps are avoided by making the threads of the adjoining colours dovetail with the bordering threads of the warp. The strength of the material is produced by this dog-tooth dovetailing process, which causes the outlines of the design to appear as if obliterated. The design itself is formed by white zig-zag lines bordered with red on both sides and so arranged as to leave between them rows of diagonally disposed squares. The centre of each square is occupied by a step-edged square design, and the intervening space is filled in by two shades of yellow also disposed step-fashion. Shoulder breadth 0,93; Length 0,5 metre.

2. A very broad poncho of simple material, not in the Gobelins style, only the lower yellow scolloping has been woven in afterwards. The edge is adorned with narrow fringes. The coloured design consists of two parts. In the upper portion comprising nearly the whole dress broad red and narrower stripes run downwards, and at their lower ends these are cut off obliquely, so as alternately to face the central seam. Thus are produced pointed step-edged scollops into which the plain yellow lower portion is dovetailed. Shoulder breadth 0,90; Length 0,8 metre.

3. A similar but much shorter garment, quite plain but for a row of step-edged squares, half yellow half green, across the shoulders. Neck and arm holes are sewed round with bright binding. Shoulder breadth 0,80; Length 0,8 metre.

4. Dress in form and design like Fig. 2, but of stronger and more uniform material. The pattern on the stripes partly represents animal heads as in Fig. 1. of Plate 67a. Each stripe consists of two narrow portions, in which the figures are worked in opposite directions. Thus the design appears as yellow on a red ground in one, and red on a yellow ground in the other, causing one half of the stripe to seem bright and the other dark. And as in the adjoining stripes the corresponding portions face each other, the intervening red ground is alternately bordered by two bright and two dark strips. Shoulder breadth 0,89; Length 0,6 metre.

PLATE 36.

SIMPLE WOOLLEN GARMENTS.
(⅓ of the natural size.)

The many-coloured garments interwoven with work of a decorative character must have belonged to persons of distinction, unless they are to be regarded as festive robes. On ordinary occasions simpler working clothes were undoubtedly worn, and such are in fact also frequently found in the graves. Two kinds may be distinguished — the short poncho reaching to the hips, and a longer garb, a species of shirt reaching half way down the thigh.

Fig. 1. A large black woollen shirt with six narrow vertical stripes; the central seam worked as an ornament. Breadth across the shoulders 0,86 metre; length 0,86.

2. A child's shirt of the same description, with brown insertion interwoven. Shoulder breadth 0,51 metre; length 0,8.

3. A child's black poncho, with fringe ornament. Shoulder breadth 0,85 metre; length 0,8.

4. A brown poncho with black border. Shoulder breadth 0,86 metre; length 0,6.

5. A small red poncho, of a loosely woven material. Shoulder breadth 0,81 metre; length 0,86.

6. A small, yellow poncho of a coarse texture, with black fringed border. The seams worked with thick, yellow thread in an ornamental style. Shoulder breadth 0,8 metre; length 0,8.

PLATE 37.

GARMENTS OF WOOL AND OF COTTON WITH WOOLLEN PATTERNS.
(⅕ of the natural size.)

Fig. 1. Large poncho woven of woollen warp and cotton weft, and embellished with uniform narrow red and yellow stripes. The garment is remarkably broad across the shoulders and of considerable height. Like the following ponchos it is made of two pieces, and has slits for inserting both arms and head. — Shoulder-breadth = 1.30; Height = 0.89 meter.

2. Small poncho with broad yellow and black stripes running in the direction of the woollen warp. The weft is formed of stout cotton threads, giving a rep-like appearance to the fabric. — Shoulder-breadth = 0.80; Height = 0.90 meter.

3. Half of a small woollen poncho. The red material woven of a plain linen-like texture is intersected by a broad strip of another texture, whose colours are confined exclusively to the warp, and whose ornamentation is effected by the application of a double warp. The richly distributed pattern of this strip is produced by the warp thread lying free on alternately broader and narrower spaces, according as they pass over one or more weft threads. In connection with such a delicately executed distribution of the pattern and of the colour effects, this technique reveals a high development of the art, and the present sample may surely be regarded as one of the most perfect achievements of simple hand-weaving. The design is formed by variegated waving and indented lines uniformly interlocked, running parallel together in an oblique direction, and converging at an acute angle along the edges of the vertical stripes. Only at the lower end of the fabric faces are interwoven, as in the border, Plate 58, without however modifying the general effect of the design. On the reverse the threads are more loosely gathered up, so that here the pattern is rendered less distinct. — Shoulder-breadth of the whole garment = 0.80; Height = 0.90 meter.

4. Half of a larger cotton and woollen poncho. In the brown material yellow and red lines mark off broad strips, whose surfaces are disposed in dove-tailed figures filling the whole space and formed by ascending and descending lines graded like flights of steps. In the red-edged strips the lower figures are executed in yellow wool, in the yellow-edged on the contrary in red wool. The garment is finished off below with a wide woollen border designed in bright colours. — Shoulder-breadth of the whole poncho = 0.90; Height = 0.90 meter.

5. Poncho with sleeves. The disproportion between the shoulder-breadth and height is increased by the attached sleeves. In the thin almost gauze-like cotton fabric indented meanders disposed in rows and executed in coloured wool form the ornamentation, which is continued along the sleeves. — Shoulder-breadth without the sleeves = 0.80; Height = 0.80 sleeve-length = 0.30 meter.

PLATE 38.

SIMPLE COTTON GARMENTS.

(¼ of the natural size.)

Fig. 1. Long, shirt-like garment of a very strong striped coloured material. It consists of two parts so stitched together as to leave an opening for the head in the middle of the seam. It is also sewed on both sides up to the openings for the arms. Two damaged places on the right side had been mended with brown yarn while the garment was still in use. The large hole in the left half is due to mouldering in the grave. The hem worked with a needle forms a durable finish below.

2. Short, shirt-like sleeved garment, characterised by great breadth of shoulders, which when worn must have caused it to fall down on the arms. The only ornament of this simple article of dress consists of a border of elegant open work with short fringes. The sleeves are sewed on.

3. Corresponds in form and quality of material with Fig. 1, and here also two damaged places have been darned with brown thread. Besides the narrow hem woven on, the garment also shows a brown fringed border sewed on.

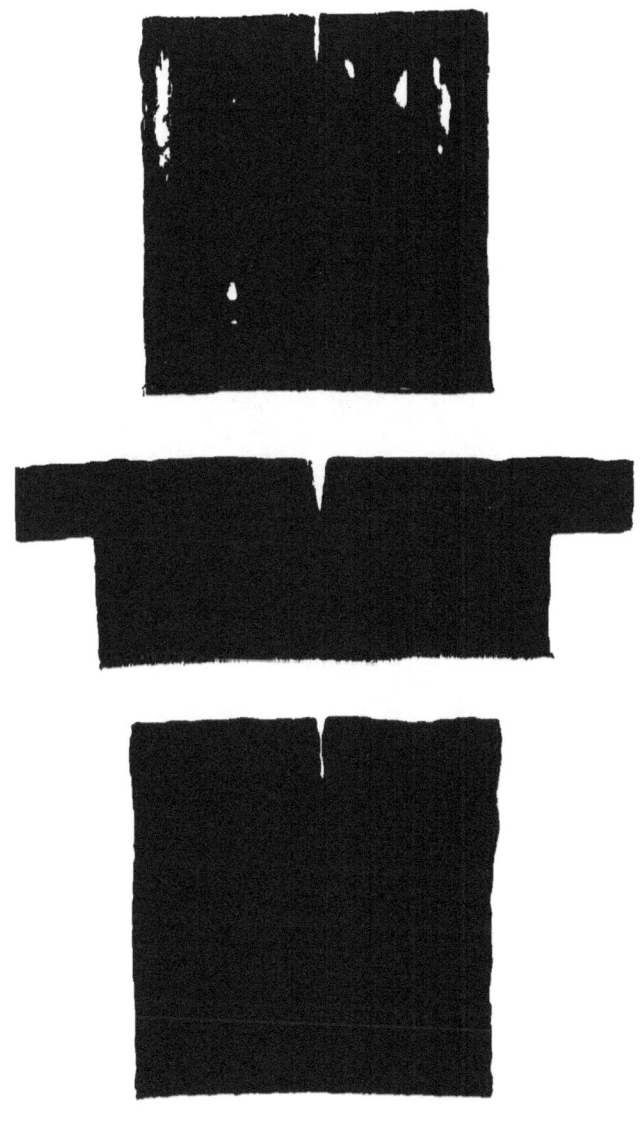

PLATE 39.

PAINTED COTTON GARMENT.

A shirt-like garment, the closely woven white cotton material of which is painted over and over with dark and light brown designs.

Fig. 1. Represents the front, on the upper portion of which a triangular space on the breast remains intact, while the rest is adorned with obliquely disposed stripes and birds. The highly conventional figures of the birds are so arranged between the stripes that the bright ground exactly reproduces the same figure as the design itself. We thus see in one and the same stripe both a dark design on a light ground, and a light design on a dark ground. The stripes meet in the centre of the garment at obtuse angles, and here are three fantastic faces disposed vertically above each other. An elegant woollen tissue has been introduced as an ornament in the lower hem.

The drawings seem to be executed with a free hand.

2. The back presents an imitation of a "feather garment". On a dark ground are raised large bright-coloured feathers covering the whole surface in horizontally disposed rows. In the small dark right angles, which remain free between the quills, there may still be detected the remains of an ornamentation apparently representing human features.

Shoulder-breadth 0.28 metres. Height 1.08 metre.

PLATE 40.

VARIOUS KINDS OF GARMENTS.
(¼ of the natural size.)

Here are grouped together such garments as are distinguished from the ordinary finds either through their shape, preparation or material employed.

Fig. 1. Large thin brown woollen robe in several places damaged by decay in the grave. It consists, not, like those previously described, of two halves sewed together, but of a single piece, the two narrow sides of which are stitched up to the small openings for the arms. These, as well as the space for the neck, are furnished with a very strong many-coloured edging. The lower extremity of the dress is edged with a woollen border, whose rich design is of very frequent recurrence with slight modifications (Pl. 66a, Fig. 1; Pl. 69, Fig. 5). The finish is formed by a short, interrupted fringe, of denticulated pattern.

The great width across the chest, as in Plate 37, Fig. 1, presents a striking contrast to the other specimens here figured. When gathered together in wearing, it must have fallen in rich folds down nearly to the knees.

2. Cotton garment of uniformly open work, made of two pieces. The design, which however survives only in a few places, was formed by obliquely disposed stripes of brown and blue interlocked meandering lines. The broad squamous tabs are woven directly on.

3. A light woollen garment in two pieces. The material was not woven of brown yarn, but dyed brown when finished. Thereby are conditioned many peculiarities of the pattern, which consists of bright spots disposed on a dark ground in somewhat irregular rows of zig-zag and meandering lines. These brighter spots were produced by slightly raising the material in each case, and firmly enveloping it in a thread, whereby the pigment was prevented from penetrating. The piece was not plunged in the dye until all the places intended to appear as spots had been so protected. To the same process is due the dark central speck shown in each spot. The disposition of the design in the garment imitates that of the woven pattern, the flat pattern of the broad upper part being edged by a border.

4. Long, shirt-like cotton garment. The material is composed of white and brown yarn so woven together, that the brown prevails on one, the white on the other side of the elegant diagonal pattern. To both of the two parts forming the dress the yellow border is directly woven on so accurately, that its rich design is nowhere interrupted at the seams.

5. Feather garment. A long, shirt-like coarse cotton robe adorned with feathers sewed on to both sides. The front shows four white fields enclosed by brown and metallic green lustrous feathers. A trimming of longer feathers may have served as a sort of fringe-like finish below. The back is simply trimmed with large, white feathers. The strings visible above are the detached edgings of the opening for the neck.

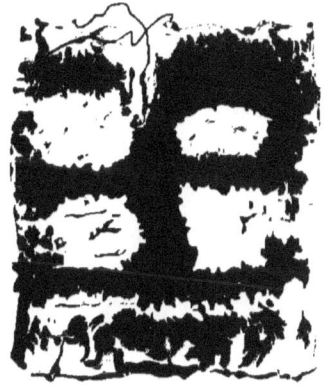

PLATE 41.

MATERIALS FOR ROBES OF THE TALARIA TYPE.

(¹/₇ of the natural size.)

While the use of most of the dress materials may easily be conjectured, those figured on plates 41—3 as for „talaria" or long flowing robes, leave some doubt as to their application and meaning. The band introduced on one of the two narrow sides of the strip of cloth, often several yards long, doubtless served apparently to fasten it round the body. But whether it was worn on the head, round the shoulders or waist, whether it fell down as a train or was wound round the body, or what rank it indicated if any, are points on which the discoveries hitherto made throw no light. We do not even know whether it was worn by men or women or by both. Probably the only hint is afforded by the illustration on plate 101. Here we see attached to the helmet of the central figure a long piece of cloth, which flows down and may perhaps be taken as a garment of the „talaria vestimenta" type. If so the prominent position occupied by the figure makes it very probable that this is a mark of high military rank.

The types figured on the three plates show the variety, size and ornamentation of these robes, which have been found in great abundance, and which constantly present the same form. Most of the specimens were taken from the group of graves indicated by figure 9 on the plan, plate 1.

1. Brown, loosely woven woollen material with strip attached, which also seems to have served as a band for fastening the dress. The strip is tastefully interwoven with a winding graduated design in red with yellow border.
2. White undyed cotton material. Sewed on the upper end is a delicate brown striped pattern, the irregular execution of which is noteworthy. On both the longer edges may be recognised folds, which seem due to the circumstance that originally either the whole striped material or at least both sides were folded lengthwise.
3. White unornamented cotton fabric with distinct traces of having been folded lengthwise. The band is retained in its original length and twist.
4. White cotton material with yellow and red woollen rosettes in appliqué. Traces of folding lengthwise. Band as originally knotted, but torn off on one side. Mildew spots. The rosettes had partly fallen away, but the stitching was still perceptible, so that nothing has here been added except the colouring.
5. Simple robe of the talaria type, formed of three narrow stripes, of which the middle one is white, the two side ones brown. The band is absent.

PROPORTIONS:

	Length.	Breadth.
Fig. 1.	1,08 metre.	0,80 metre.
„ 2.	1,6 „	0,... „
„ 3.	1,5 „	0,08 „
„ 4.	1,21 „	0,85 „
„ 5.	1 m	1,5

PLATE 42.

LARGE ROBES OF THE TALARIA TYPE.
(⅛ of the natural size.)

Fig. 1. Piece of a flowing garment, formed of diverse coloured broad and narrow stripes, each separately woven. As in Fig. 5 of Plate 41, here are clearly shown the seams joining the several stripes.

The coloured stripes were symmetrically disposed; but in the present specimen the outer stripes to the left are missing. Both the brown and blue are of wool, but woven very loosely almost like a veil. A durable finish is effected above and below by hemming the narrow length of the piece.

2. White cotton forms the material of this simple robe, which is distinguished by its great length. A long broad band of like description serves to fasten it to the waist. Both on the band and the cloth may be observed the already mentioned traces of folding on the length (Plate 41, Fig. 1). The rents shown in the material, which is much decayed in parts, have also arisen mainly in the creases of the folds.

3. Flowing robe with broad woollen trimming. For this style of garment a brown loosely woven woollen material seems to have been usually preferred. The woollen border, whose bright colours are well preserved, is attached as an ornamental finish only to the bottom, not to the top end, as was the case in the corresponding piece, Fig. 1 of the previous Plate. Thanks to the good preservation of this trimming, the disposition of its pattern, the grouping of the colours and the technical execution are all displayed to the best possible advantage.

The border consists of a broad central piece and two side stripes. The pattern of the former is formed by rows of diamond figures enframed in undulating lines. Both of the side stripes are interwoven with a yellow woollen band. At the upper end of the garment the band serving to fasten it has been preserved in its original length, but on one side only.

PLATE 43.

ORNAMENTED ROBES OF THE TALARIA TYPE WITH ACCOMPANYING TRIMMINGS.

(⅓ of the natural size.)

The ornamentation of these garments is usually restricted to a strip at the end of the long self-coloured fabric. It consists mostly of a more or less wide edging of some richly coloured Gobelins material. Of these trimmings a large number are distinguished by the uniformity of their form, colour, and disposition of the pattern, as is clearly shown in Figs. 1—4 of this Plate and on Plate 61. Each of these pieces of trimming consists of a central portion with two flap-like attachments on either side, whose projecting lower end nearly always represents a face. Yellow woollen fringes serve as an edging. On its lower side the central portion mostly shows a reentering angle, a conventional insertion which in other pieces is at least indicated in the design. Details of the material and pattern must be supplied from Plates 61—63.

Fig. 1. Piece of trimming. The pattern of the central portion consists of two systems of many-coloured stripes converging at an unusually sharp angle. The ornament of the several stripes is a repeatedly recurring bird figure. The two flap-like side-pieces are distinguished from those of Figs. 1—4, Plate 62a by oblique striping.

2. Piece of trimming, whose pattern consist of a few obliquely disposed stripes striking at a sharp angle against another from the opposite side, so that here the obtuse-angled incision is edged with scalloped stripes parallel with its sides. The design of the stripes is composed of alternating yellow, red and black meander-lines. A small remnant of the cotton robe has been preserved attached to the trimming. Here the flap-like side-pieces are replaced by yellow fringed borders.

3. Trimming, in which central and side pieces are all woven in one, although the latter are sharply defined by their different pattern. The pattern of the central piece is formed by numerous meander-lines disposed diagonally. The angular insertion peculiar to these trimmings is here produced by reserving the yellow design in the red ground.

4. Instead of the trimming we have here narrow strands directly sewed to the cotton material of the talaria. Each of the side pieces reproduces the hook pattern in three parallel stripes. The fringed edging is limited to the semi-circular prolongations.

5. Trimming of a very wide robe of the talaria type. It is made up of two halves, through the junction of which the systems of diagonal stripes are brought together at right angles. During the preparation of the symmetrical pieces care was taken to mark off a large angular insertion by reserving the brown corners. A portion of the girdle for fastening to the body is still preserved. The pattern is given on a larger scale in Fig. 2, Plate 63.

6. Woollen talaria, whose Gobelins trimming is figured on Plate 62.

7. Cotton talaria, in its upper part decorated with rosettes attached, and so arranged as to allow the inserted angle to be here also detected (Plate 44, Fig. 4); in the lower section six parallel white fringed borders are sewed on.

8. Trimming of the talaria type in passementerie work. Semi-circular disks with figurative representations (Plate 60a, Fig. 2) form a finish to long pendant bands. The tie at the upper end must have served to fasten it possibly to the head.

PLATE 43a.

DRESS MATERIALS.

(Figs. 1, 2 and 3/4 of the natural size.)

Fig. 1. Large cotton cloth with corner ornaments; the texture is fine and extremely uniform. The corner ornaments form step triangles, the two corners facing each other diagonally being worked in red, the other two in black wool. The pattern is made up of small rhombs, the edge of each corner being moreover stitched round in diverse colours. Length 2.30, width 1.45 meter.

2. Triangular cotton cloth so loosely woven as to represent open lattice work. The piece was made in square form and folded on the diagonal. A narrow figured Gobelins border is sewed to the two short sides, where the connection had to be made between the two halves loosely covering each other.

3. Brown cotton cloth with border woven to the upper and lower end of the warp. The warp threads are joined in threes to form a warp thread for the border, the warp thus formed being but partly filled in, and lying partly free. The middle stripe shows a pattern executed in stout yellow and red woollen threads, which last lie loose on large spaces. Parallel with this wide central stripe are narrow stripes of cotton thread passed through the open warp. To one side of the piece is also sowed a coarsely woven strip terminating in fringes.

4. Cotton cloth made up of four pieces sewed together. Two of the pieces have a brown ground with interwoven white design, one a blue ground with brown design, and the fourth a green ground with brown design. In all four the pattern corresponds exactly, mainly repeating the outlines of the design shown in the Gobelins piece Pl. 56, Fig. 3. The threads are taken up in twos both for the weft and the warp, by which the design is effected. A variegated woollen border is woven as a finish to the upper as well as to the lower end of the warp; but while one border is narrow, showing a simple hook ornament, as in Pl. 104, Fig. 10, the other is nearly as broad again and embellished with an intricate hook ornament. Although each of the four pieces with the accompanying borders was woven separately, the pattern is so accurately carried out that no break is noticed in any of the seams, not excepting that of the border; and so carefully are the four pieces adjusted that scarcely a single seam is perceptible, the whole cloth appearing rather as if woven in one piece.

5. Small blue and white check cotton cloth. The large squares are edged with narrow stripes, and to the sides of the warp ends are woven woollen borders, whose warp is formed by the warp-threads of the cloth taken in twos. The proper finish of the warp is however effected by two stout cotton strands which again are passed through the loops. The warp of the piece consists of stout threads, while in the weft fine threads lie in twos side by side.

6. Brown check cotton stuff. In each square is worked in coloured wool a quadruped, whose long neck and head are turned backwards. Green, red, yellow and black rows alternate diagonally, only in the central diagonal row the alternate figures are green and white. The middle piece is surrounded on all sides by a row of empty squares and an edge of more closely disposed stripes.

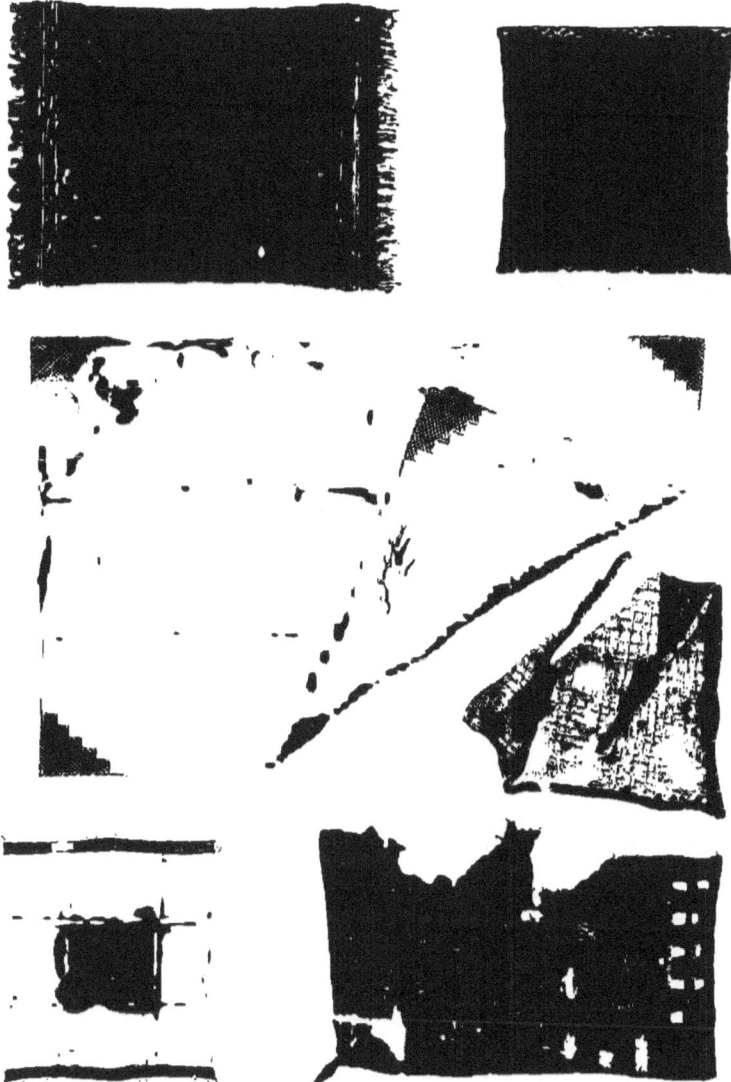

PLATE 44.

LOIN-GIRDLES AND WOOLLEN CLOTHS.
(¼ of the natural size.)

As the last and simplest class of garments must be mentioned the loin-girdles (Figs. 2—5), which appear from the sepulchral deposits to have been worn in pre-Spanish times, and were often seemingly the only article of dress. The purpose of the two large woollen pieces (Figs. 1 and 6) cannot be clearly determined.

Fig. 1. Brightly ornamented woollen cloth, consisting of three separately woven pieces. Each of these has the form of an equilateral right-angled triangle, so that when put together with the catheti in a line they form three-fourths of a square surface. Whether the fourth piece completing the square ever existed is uncertain. The coarse cotton warp of the woollen material runs in each piece parallel with one cathetus, while the ends of the warp form at the hypothenuses the fringes of the indented meandering ornament. The pattern, executed in the Gobelins manner, is with slight deviations the same in all three pieces. It consists of a series of stripes running parallel with the hypothenuses of the triangles, each stripe being disposed by a graduated meandering line into two parts of equal size but differently coloured, and interlocked hook-fashion one in the other. The right angles of the large triangular pieces are white, thus producing in the centre of the whole material a light surface, while the edge displays the darkest shade. It is noteworthy that in the central piece the several members of the meandering fringe increase in size towards the middle.

Besides the specimen here figured one other triangular piece only was found in another part of the Necropolis, resembling it in design and colour.

2. Loin-girdle. Long woollen fringes, forming the essential part of the garment, are attached to a band executed in the Gobelins style, and embellished with three figures (Plate 65, Fig. 3). The fringes consist of thick woollen threads loosely twisted into strings. A plaited cord serves to fasten the whole to the body.

3. Loin-girdle, wider and more richly executed than Fig. 2. The broad red band is disposed by light stripes into a number of rectangles, within which may be detected the remains of a coloured ornament. Here the girdle is formed by a cotton strip.

4. Simple loin-girdle. Round a string made of Agave (Cabuya) fibre are wound the fringes, whose tips are adorned with little feathers.

5. Simple loin-girdle, wider than Fig. 4; the fringes disposed in a central yellow and two red stripes.

6. Part of a material composed of loosely woven strips. In the interior of many mummy packs were found such cloths, always carefully folded up, but never under conditions which might have revealed their purpose. The frequency alone of their occurrence seems to imply that they served as articles of dress. The cloths, mostly very long compared with their breadth, occur in all sizes from pieces scarcely half a meter long to others three meters long by 70 centimeters wide. The several strips of which they consist are loosely woven with wide meshes, so that they often look more like a net than a woven fabric. The black threads, formed of long hair lightly twisted together, are thick and coarse, and the threads lie somewhat closer together only in the red woollen strips, which usually form one hem of the cloth. In several pieces besides this red band there occurs a second woollen strip of a red or violet colour inserted between the wide-meshed portions.

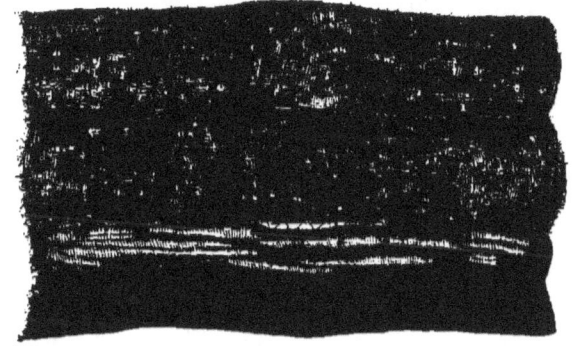

VI.

TEXTILE FABRICS.

(PLATES 45—71.)

The purpose of this section is to give a general picture of the materials found in Ancon, in other words to disclose the development reached by the weaver's art in this part of the Peruvian empire.

Besides the garments, it was necessary to figure a considerable number of woven pieces in order fully to illustrate the diversity of design, the manner of arranging the colours, the various weaving processes and their embellishment by means of coloured patterns often introduced by special methods of binding, lastly the ornamentation of the materials with borders, trimmings and passementerie sewed on or to the piece. In the selection of the available material preference was given to the more highly ornamented specimens, not however to the neglect of simple unadorned fabrics, as well as knitting, plaiting and network.

The gorgeous effect of garments prepared with such materials may be best appreciated from a few specimens, whose brilliant colours have scarcely suffered perceptible loss, and may even be surmised from such pieces as have faded in the course of centuries from the mould of the grave.

In the ornamentation we are struck by the frequent use of human and animal figures, as well as by the absence of motives borrowed from the vegetable kingdom. By a skilful use of colour effects a great diversity of designs has been developed from an essentially limited store of forms, as may be perceived from the study of the meander and other familiar motives.

In the preparation of the reproductions the greatest possible fidelity to the originals has been the first consideration. The texture of the fabric is reproduced most exactly by a photographic picture transferred by the phototype process. The colours have been most carefully shaded after the original pieces, in order to give facsimiles of the fabrics, as far as this was possible by means of chromo-lithography. Hence the Plates show the materials exactly as they were found, without any attempt at restoring the original form or colour.

The textiles are arranged according to the style of costume for which they were used, the series beginning with jerkins or smocks of the poncho type, followed by the trimmings of garments of the talaria type, and ending with the trimmings of simple cotton garments and of simple cotton cloths. The borders and border-like ornaments, which were partly found separated from the materials, form a division apart. At the end are brought together some self-coloured loosely woven fabrics remarkable for their peculiar texture.

Within these main divisions the several pieces are grouped according to the material used in their preparation, the heavy woollen stuffs being followed by the lighter cotton fabrics. But it was impossible to strictly adhere to this grouping on the Plates, where numerous transpositions were necessitated by the technical difficulties of reproduction.

A survey of the more important ornamental forms is presented by Plates 102—104 in the twelfth Part appended to the third Volume.

The coloured Plates were painted by Fräulein Martha Hennig from photographic originals; the photographs and the phototypes used in the chromolithographic process were prepared in Herr Frisch's establishment, Berlin.

PLATES OF PART VI.

a. Pieces of Woollen Garments.

50.	Gobelins fabric ornamented in superior style	Plate 45
51.	Counterpart of Material on previous Plate	" 46
52.	Half of a fine Woollen Garment	" 47
53.	Richly ornamented Woollen Dress	" 48
54.	Sumptuous Garment of a Mummy	" 49
55.	Tapestry with figures of Warriors	" 50
56.	Gobelins Materials with Human figures — Portions of Woollen Garments	" 51
57.	Gobelins Fabrics with Human and Animal figures — Portions of Woollen Garments .	" 52
58.	Three Gobelins Pieces with Human figures — Portions of Woollen Garments	" 53
59.	Figured Gobelins with Geometrical and Animal designs — Portions of Woollen Garments	" 53a
60.	Dress Materials with Geometrical Patterns	" 54
61.	Gobelins Stuffs with Geometrical Patterns and Animal figures — Parts of Woollen Garments	" 55
62.	Dress Materials and Borderings	" 55a
63.	Woollen Gobelins fabrics with Animal figures	56

b. Cotton Stuffs ornamented with Wool.

64.	Boldly ornamented dress Materials	" 57
65.	Ornamental Cotton Garment with Woollen border	" 58
66.	Dress Materials horizontally striped	59
67.	Cotton dress Materials	59a

c. Passementerie Work.

68.	Dress Materials with Passementerie trimmings	" 60
69.	Passementerie Work	" 60a

d. Trimmings for Robes of the Talaria Type.

70.	Border of a Robe of the Talaria Type	" 61
71.	Woollen border of a flowing Garment	" 62
72.	Trimmings of robes of the Talaria Type — Woollen Materials	" 62a
73.	Borders of flowing Garments — Ornamented Woollen Corner pieces	" 63

e. Corners and trimmings of simple Cotton fabrics and dresses.

74.	Ornamented Corners	Plate 64
75.	Cotton Cloths with ornamental Corners and Hem	„ 64a
76.	Ornamental Hems of small Cotton cloths	„ 64b
77.	Woollen trimmings of Cotton garments	„ 65
78.	Cotton Materials with Woollen trimmings	„ 65a

f. Borderings.

79.	Broad Gobelins Woollen Borderings	„ 66
80.	Borders and border-like fabrics	„ 66a
81.	Borderings and Sleeve trimmings	„ 67
82.	Borderings of Garments	„ 67a
83.	Woollen Borders of Cotton garments	„ 67b
84.	Woollen Dress Borderings	„ 68
85.	Border-like Woollen fabrics	„ 68a
86.	Woollen Borders and Cotton dress Materials	„ 68b
87.	Woollen Borders	„ 69
88.	Pieces of insertion and Woollen Band	„ 69a
89.	Sundry pieces of weaving	„ 69b
90.	Diverse kinds of simple dress Materials	„ 69c

g. Loosely woven net-like Materials.

91.	Loosely woven and reticulated Stuffs	„ 70
92.	Loosely woven and reticulated Cotton stuffs	„ 70a
93.	Cotton stuffs reticulated and ornamented with Needlework	„ 71

PLATE 45.

GOBELINS FABRIC ORNAMENTED IN SUPERIOR STYLE.
(²/₃ of the natural size.)

Amongst all the dress materials obtained in the Ancon Necropolis those figured on this and the following plate are specially distinguished both by the grandeur and uniform character of the design, and by a careful and delicate execution even in the minutest details.

The whole surface of the piece is devoted to the representation of a highly decorated head. The pale red full face occupies a comparatively small space, and is enframed in a green and yellow fancy border, which causes it to stand sharply out from the dark red ground. Above the face rises the head-dress enclosed in a border on blue ground, and from this projecting cover springs a shade-like superstructure expanding upwards, and formed by a system of stripes laid parallel over each other. Beneath this superstructure two obliquely striped bands, projecting from the head-dress itself, expand abruptly downwards, ending with horizontal edges, to the four sides of which are attached light blue tassels. In the high head-dress two parts may be distinguished — one consisting of narrow horizontal stripes, the other composed of broad borders broken off towards the sides, and for which the first serves as a support. The borders display a great variety of design. Of the head-dress, which for want of space appears cut off on both sides, the outer lines are vandyked in black and white and fall down right and left to protect the head. The effect of the design is judiciously enhanced by black lines between the fancy borders. The inside of the cap-like covering, which supports the superstructure, is divided by diagonal bands into square fields, whose dark ground shows conventional little birds.

The space with red ground remaining near the face is interwoven with small figures, which have no direct relation to the large head. Of these the largest standing out to the right of the observer are two human figures, whose head-dress agrees with that of the large head, as is still evident from the outlines. One of the figures is in full length, the other short and stout, as conditioned by the space to be filled in. The smallest inserted ornaments would also seem to represent living beings. In the lowest corner are visible six black stripes ending in yellow tips. The left and narrower side of the material is too badly preserved to enable the details to be recognised.

Noteworthy are the upper corners remaining unoccupied right and left of the head-dress. In each case the space is filled in with a large and a small human figure, slight differences in which show that one was intended for a man, the other for a woman. The head-dress, here quite perfect, enables us better to understand the large central representation, as do also Plates 46, 51, 53, 100 and Plate 33 suggestively.

The warp laid bare at several places consists of strong cotton threads, the woof of the finest wool.

The materials both of this piece and of that represented on Plate 46 were rudely stitched together at their upper ends, and were found wrapped up in a cloth with other fabrics, as parting gifts for a badly preserved mummy in one of the graves lying between Nos 9 and 11 of the plan, Plate 1.

PLATE 46.

COUNTERPART OF MATERIAL ON PREVIOUS PLATE.

(⅔ of the natural size.)

The central portion of the dark red surface is occupied by a large self-contained design flanked on both sides by numerous human figures. It consists of a red, club-shaped thickened stem, the top-end of which is enclosed by a black octagonal corona, below which a black and gold fancy garment spreads out terminating right and left with a peculiar palisade-like finish. The red stem is decorated with a row of smaller designs — a human figure on the broadened base surmounted by three squares in green, yellow and black, which are disposed vertically in the narrow shaft. The centre of the upper octagonal expansion is filled by a larger human face, with an imposing head-dress, which is surrounded by smaller figures and thus occupies to a certain extent the centre of the whole picture. The black, octagonal corona is also filled with small cuneiform ornaments, which follow the outlines of the red, inner octagon. The upper side of the black octagon supports a light-coloured strip, whose obliquely bent ends terminate with two goblet-shaped figures, which may be taken either as supports, or as a species of tassels. Above this stripe rises an irregular five-sided piece, whose black ground is filled with squares grouped in diagonal order, while the outer border is decorated with yellow and red faces. The interior of the squares shows red figures of birds on a yellow ground, and the black intervening spaces are interwoven with small white rings.

The remaining space on either side of the central ornament is animated by a number of small figures betraying great freedom of treatment. We feel that the artist is constantly yielding to the impulse of the moment, designing, so to say, with the yarn and adapting each separate figure to the available space. In the lower right corner is a large vase resting on a stand, and in its wide mouth balancing a triangular strip with horizontal lines. In the upper right corner are the remains of some larger ornamental work. All the other figures represent human forms, disposed and decorated in exquisite style. By the side of these designs, whose human character is revealed at the first glance, there are others reduced almost to conventional ornaments, whose meaning it would be difficult to conjecture but for the transitional forms here, as it happens, frequently occurring. In the upper right corner is a human figure with a large head-dress (Plates 45, 47, 50, 51, 53, 65), and near him a seated figure with turban-shaped hat and two projecting plumes or cognizances, and holding in its hand a pouch or club. The up-curved train-like appendage recalls the design on Plate 49. The same figure, reduced almost to a mere ornament, recurs several times again in diversely modified form.

Above the already mentioned vase is a large head of the idol type, at whose side is figured a draped Indian, in a half kneeling attitude almost of adoration.

On the left side may be mentioned a draped figure in profile with a very full head of hair, and in its outstretched hands holding some lengthy object. Immediately above is a large head with suspended ornaments and with the feet directly attached.

A few only of the more noteworthy designs could here be specified; but all challenge serious consideration, giving as they do numerous indications of the peculiar artistic development of the ancient Peruvians, and rendering possible the interpretation of many otherwise unintelligible ornaments.

PLATE 47.

HALF OF A FINE WOOLLEN GARMENT.
(⅓ of the natural size.)

Right half of a richly ornamented dress of the poncho type, distinguished by the trimming round the arm-hole suggestive of a short sleeve. Like most garments of this class, it is made up of a number of narrow strips in the Gobelins style. The insertion, which is the broadest of these strips, is an artistic piece of weaving, in which faces with head-dress and stand are arranged in a row between horizontal stripes of various patterns. The next and narrower band, four times repeated in the illustration, shows the frequently recurring graduated check pattern, and jointly with an interrupted edging forms the border of the insertion. The edging consists of two closely woven side stripes connected together by a string of loose woollen threads disposed in zig-zag fashion.

But while the narrow strips run uniformly over the whole surface from top to bottom, the central insertion consists of two pieces joined together by an oblique seam, and in such a way that the figures of the one have their heads turned upwards, and those of the other downwards.

The ground of the ornamental stripes shows numerous gaps, which are due to the corroding effect of the black dye, by which the wool is easily destroyed. This gives a thinner appearance than it originally possessed to the dress, whose bright red colour is agreeably toned by five others introduced into the design.

In striking contrast to the perfect finish of the work, and to the delicacy and uniform texture of its tissue, are the few careful stitches and coarse threads binding together the several strips. They almost give the impression of a later and hastily executed mending.

To keep within the limits of the plate the lowest hem of the garment had to be turned up, as clearly shown in the illustration.

PLATE 48.

RICHLY ORNAMENTED WOOLLEN DRESS.

(Fig. 1 ⸺ ¹/₁₀; Fig. 2 ⸺ ¹/₅ of the natural size.)

Fig. 1. The Poncho of the ancient Peruvians usually consisted of two pieces of equal size, stitched together in the middle and at the sides, with openings for head and arms. But owing to the imperfection of the looms highly decorated materials could be woven only in narrow strips. Hence Ponchos such as that here figured had to be put together of several pieces.

The two halves — the right and left — consist on the whole of two pieces of equal size symmetrically disposed; only in the middle of each half an irregularity is introduced of such a character that the separate coloured strips no longer correspond. A border is also added to the half on the right of the observer, making the shoulder breadth greater than that on the opposite side.

2. The half of the same garment on a larger scale, showing the ornamentation and texture of the material.

A ribbed fabric disposed in coloured horizontal bands forms the centre-piece, whose several coloured stripes separating the larger spaces are provided with elegant patterns. Here are repeated both an S-shaped design interlaced one with another, and on the broader stripes an animal form reduced to a purely ornamental type. On both sides of the central piece are introduced broad yellow and red borders, the transition to which is effected by narrow, red braiding, such as that which serves to form the outer edge of the garment. One of the two borders, of which half alone is consequently represented, disappears about the middle of the breast, so that the opening for the head ornamented with a braid-like stitch had to be cut out of the material.

The Goblin-like texture of the borders is finer than that of the central piece, and the design essentially different. Yellow diamond-shaped figures, filling the whole breadth of the border, stand in rows one above the other. In the middle of each lozenge four animal heads meet together, advancing in couples from either side. Round the necks of these heads are stripes of the same colour vandyked in an axe-like pattern. These, as is evident from other specimens elsewhere preserved, must be regarded as conventional wings, forming the side lines of the figures. Between every two of the yellow designs are two half ornaments of diamond pattern, precisely in the same style, but of a red colour. These however are introduced in such a way that, were the border conceived as somewhat wider, rows of lozenge-shaped representations in red and yellow would follow each other close together in the direction from right to left. At the same time the design is so carried out that both coloured ornaments become interlaced, producing the effect of a yellow design on a red ground, or of a red on a yellow according as the attention is fixed at one point or another.

By the introduction of green and blue lines a transition is brought about between the two contrasting colours, so that the general effect satisfies even the critical eye.

The seams connecting the several segments are partly executed in a coarse style. Neither the length of the stitches nor the size and colour of the thread are in keeping with the delicacy and colour of the material. They are evidently hasty mendings essentially different from the careful character of the original work.

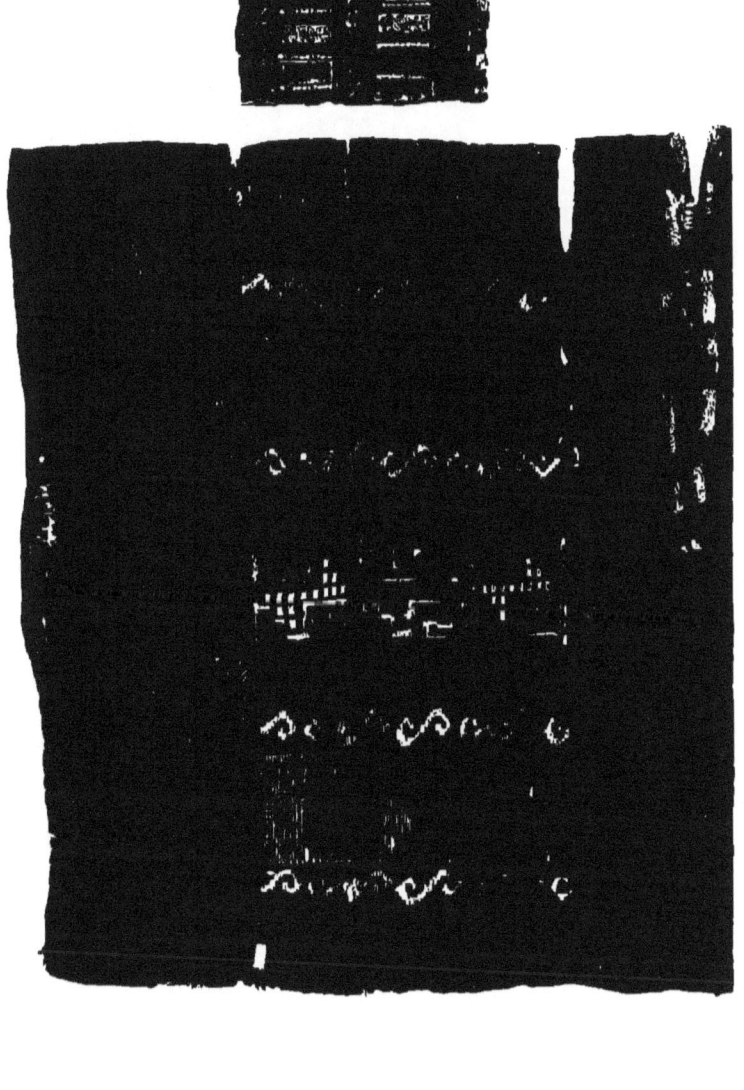

PLATE 49.

SUMPTUOUS GARMENT OF A MUMMY.

(Natural size.)

The broad yellow stripes of the fine Gobelins robe belonging to the mummy figured on Plate 16 are ornamented in the richest manner. A first glance at the confusion of white lines and bright patches of colour will not reveal the pictorial representation designed by a wonderful fancy and woven by a practised hand. The design of each stripe shows the sevenfold recurrence of two human figures, one seated, the other standing, but both conceived in the most original manner, and surrounded with diverse attributes and ornaments. Two pairs are here reproduced to illustrate the various dispositions both of the colours and attitudes.

The seated figures are drawn altogether in profile, but the standing ones in such a way that we get a front view of the bodies and a side view of the heads and legs. A comparison of both groups reveals a substantial difference in the treatment of the several members, apart altogether from the disposition of the colours. The eyes, ears and nose are partly ornamented in a way difficult to describe; but the mouth is more natural. The black hair parted behind the ears falls with the sitting figures down to the shoulders, while with the others it reaches only to the lower part of the ear. In both the arms are bent in at the elbow, and embellished with pendant ornaments. The hands of the standing figure are uniformly drawn with four fingers and the feet with three toes only, whereas with the others the hand has the full number of fingers, but the first four toes only. The nails are in all cases clearly indicated. The leg of the sitting figure is crossed by a stripe, as if to suggest the bone with its prominence at the hip-joint, while in the other figure the legs are covered by a tunic reaching nearly to the feet and fastened by a girdle. Very different is the decoration of the bodies, the most noteworthy feature in which is obviously the butterfly wing attached to the back of the seated figures.

In the other adornments differences also occur, although the two sets of figures otherwise show great analogy. Different are the fantastic head-dresses, the objects held in the hands and the surrounding ornaments. A peculiar type of decoration projecting from the lowest part of the seat is curved upwards behind the back, ending in a scarcely discernible conventional animal-head with up-turned snout. A perfectly analogous ornament, but ending in a bird's head, is attached to the toes of one of the standing figure's feet, and in fact conventional animal heads of this type frequently recur both on the head-dress, the garments and the occiput of these figures.

The figure equipped with bow and arrow is followed by a dog on foot, undoubtedly the *Canis ingae*, here apparently for the first time occurring in a pictorial illustration. On the same side with the dog a bird is also introduced just above the upper end of the club in the archer's right hand, which is embellished with a face.

The little rectangles thrown in between the limbs are apparently intended merely to fill in the spaces harmoniously. The whole is conceived and executed in a way to suggest the well known sculptures on the monolithic gate of Tiahuanaco.

PLATE 50.

TAPESTRY WITH FIGURES OF WARRIORS.
(⅔ of the natural size.)

The strip from which the piece here figured is taken, served either as a border or trimming, or else several such strips were sewn together to form the garment itself. Of both descriptions the finds in Ancon offer numerous examples, although the breadth of the strip seems more in accordance with the latter supposition.

A fine cotton warp is interwoven in the Gobelin method with diverse-coloured worsteds, but in such a way that each particular patch of colour is worked out separately. Hence the various positions of one and the same colour have no mutual connection, and both sides of the material present exactly the same picture.

On a red ground are grouped together a series of squares, each of which is enclosed in a wide frame filled in with figures. In the space thus defined a warrior is represented, in his right hand holding as a trophy a decorated head, in his left an ornamented rod. The figure is contracted, dressed in a species of shirt, and depicted with broad features, large eyes and a row of formidable teeth. The prominences right and left of the face doubtless represent the ear ornaments. The head is decked with a kind of plumed hat, and between the head and trunk is inserted a broad neck-tie. The front view of the figure shows the legs turned outwards, so that the three-toed feet point right and left. The garment, arms and legs are all adorned with diverse-coloured patterns. The upper portion of the rod grasped in the left hand is flattened out and shews a human face.

The figures which with monotonous repetition fill in the frame enclosing the chief figure, also represent human beings, tho' certainly of an extremely conventional type. The figure adorned with a plume seems to be stooping over some object resembling a chair.

The same design, with varying disposition of the colours, is repeated along the entire length of the material.

PLATE 51.

GOBELINS MATERIALS WITH HUMAN FIGURES.
PORTIONS OF WOOLLEN GARMENTS
(Natural size.)

Fig. 1. Human figures grouped in rows are woven with yellow wool into the red fabric originally apparently of a brilliant colour. The monotony produced by these constantly recurring forms is diminished by reversing the direction of the figures in profile. The human figures are strongly conventionalised. A side view was seemingly intended, as is in fact effected for the face, arm and ornaments attached to the front and back; only the peculiarly bent legs turned to the right and left are awkwardly represented in full view. The black and white eye is fixed in the middle of the square head, which is furnished with a beak-like mouth, and which merges directly in the short body arrayed in a stiff, expanded garment. A black ornament is introduced in the middle of the garment, and a blue-green stripe attached to its front angles. From the body, or more probably from the dress, there runs backwards a triangular strip attached close under the head, and showing on the under side two blue-green squares. The three-fingered hand seems to be grasping at an object hovering in front of the figure, and in form and colour somewhat harmonising with the ornament introduced beneath the back angle of the dress. But the most striking feature in these figures is the black and white scalloped and disproportionately large head-dress towering above the triangular hat set on the crown.

2. This fabric agrees in texture, ground colour and grouping of the figures in rows with the foregoing, but differs from it in as much as here the sections of the alternating rows are formed by two different designs, which are moreover separated by a narrow intervening ornamental stripe. Thus the upper row shows in profile seated figures all facing to the left. But the same figure returns in the third row facing to the right, and the same alternating disposition of these figures is observed throughout, the rows being invariably separated by lines of busts facing the observer. These busts are all executed in uniform style and colour. Above the dark face sunk into the shoulders there rises the broad band of the head-covering provided with four vertical scallopings, while four green and yellow tassels or supports form the lower finish to the body, which is merely suggested above. On both sides of each head two diagonal squares, one green and one yellow, are inserted on the dark red ground.

In the seated figures there prevails a great play of colours, whereas the forms show only slight and arbitrary deviations. The head, hands and feet are rudely figured. In the fanciful colouring of the body an anatomical style of ornamentation may perhaps be detected, such as has already been pointed out in the seated figure of Plate 49. Between every other figure there are indicated in green and yellow two objects, which can scarcely be recognised.

The narrow stripes between the rows of figures, as well as the border of the foregoing specimen show a decorative style strongly suggestive of Greek patterns.

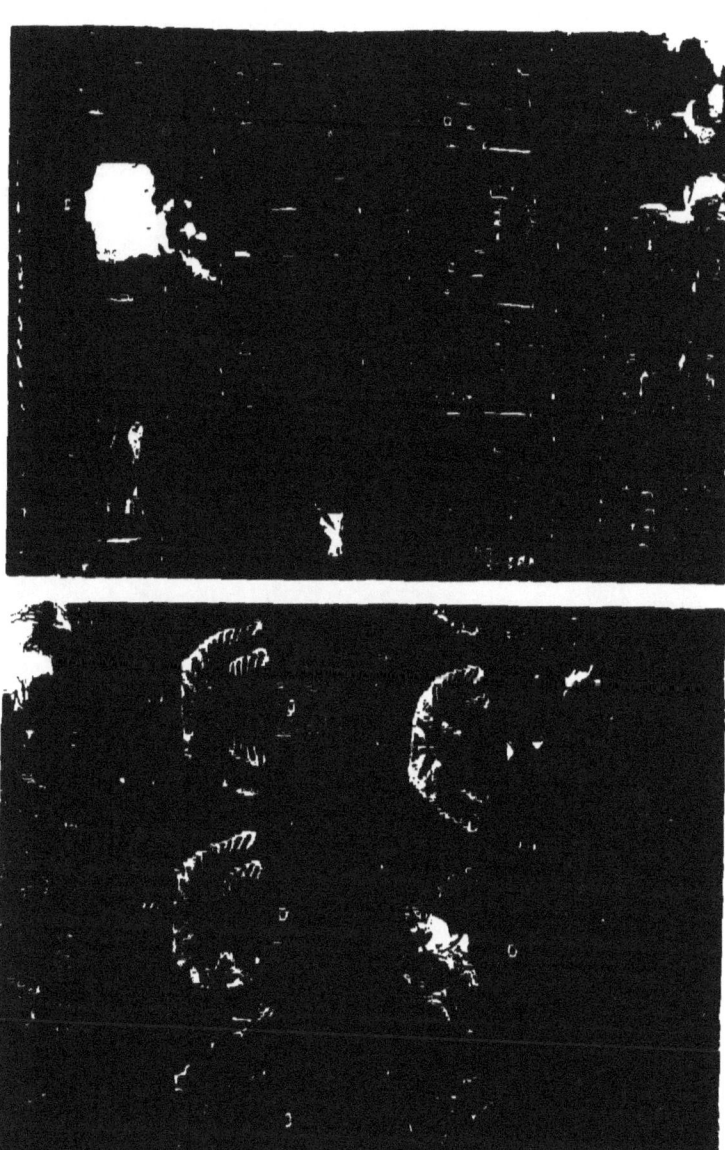

PLATE 52.

GOBELIN FABRICS WITH HUMAN AND ANIMAL FIGURES.

PORTIONS OF WOOLLEN GARMENTS.

(Fig. 1. 4 (?) Fig. 2. ⅑ of the natural size.)

Fig. 1. Fine, thick material, whose central section may probably be regarded as an attempt at a pictorial representation of some actual event. Without venturing to suggest the subject, a few peculiarities may be pointed out:

The green ornament may be conceived as a sort of canopy overshadowing a large yellow and red square seat. Beneath it is a small figure decked with a head-dress but unfortunately greatly damaged — presumably the chief personage in the scene. A carpet lies spread before the canopy. The figures acquire a bird-like appearance from the more or less open beaks, which are often of considerable length. All stretch forward a three-fingered hand attached to arms of varying length. But while most of them face to the right, those of the lowest row are reversed in the direction of a figure seated in the extreme left corner. The figure introduced between the canopy and carpet turns its head backwards either in alarm or inquiringly. On the right hem facing two smaller figures are two others also distinguished by their size and beaks. In the lower right corner a trunkless head with a hand attached hovers above another small figure. The third figure in the upper row lacks the body for which a yellow rectangle has been substituted. In other respects the decoration of the figures is pretty uniform. The front is of a bright, the back of a dark colour, and all are dressed in a garment girdled to the waist, and showing the claw-footed extremities below. The eye stands in the middle of the head, and some of the 24 figures still show a red spot in the middle of the body above the waist. The four green-edged objects are probably stools. Coloured spots and small triangles are distributed in seemingly arbitrary fashion over the surface.

The borders round the central piece present a remarkable delicacy of design and disposition of colour. The middle stripe is especially noteworthy for its ornaments of red birds on yellow ground. The design is best revealed by holding the border vertically and then following with the eye the course of the red lines.

The whole material woven in one piece formed with a symmetrical counterpart repeating the same design the front portion of a small poncho.

2. In the central piece, woven in the Gobelins style, the lower part of the space is occupied by a large bird with outspread wings, the feathers of wings and tail being merely suggested. A crest or plume appears on the head, and the beak is strongly bent. The figure had been frequently repeated, as is evident from the remains of the tail feathers on the right side. Above the bird are draped human figures, and in the left corner is a kind of urn with a black cover resembling a head.

To the central gobelins strips borders had been sewed on above and below, of which, however, the upper ones alone have been preserved. Two of these show a recumbent meander, while the third is divided into small sections with constantly recurring ornaments. The black fancy hem is formed by turning over and sewing down the edge.

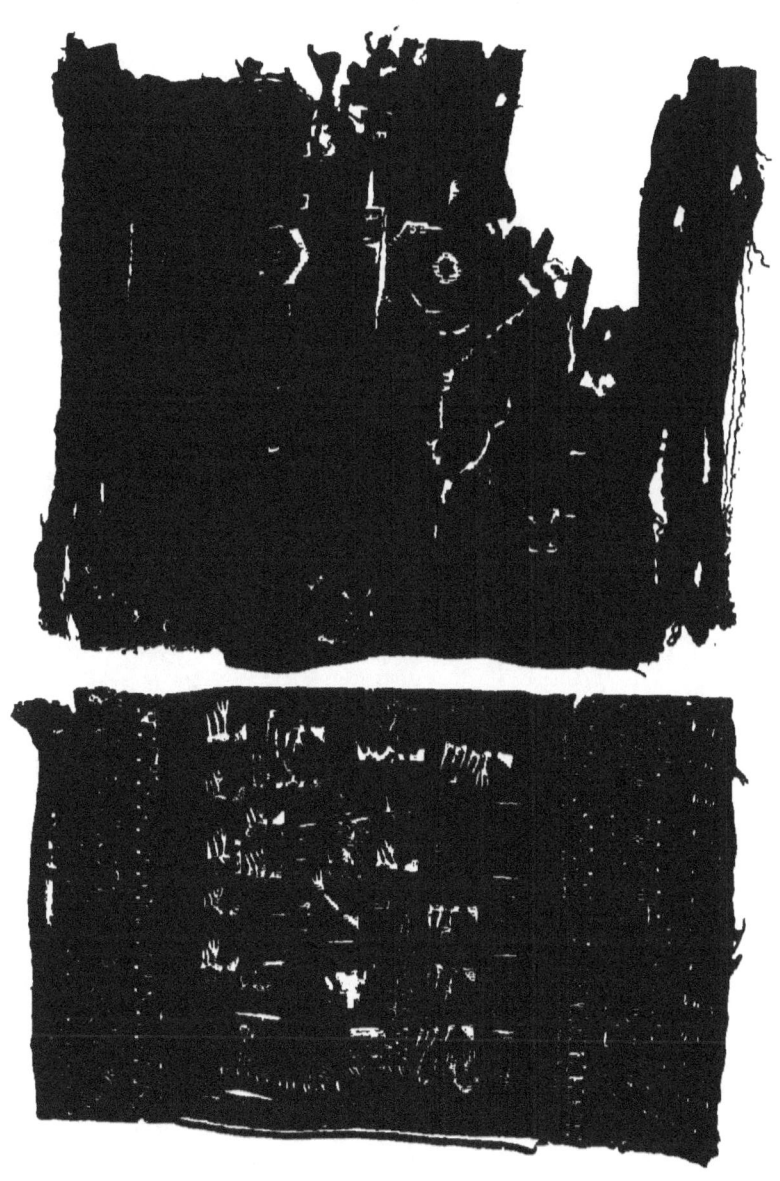

PLATE 53.

THREE GOBELINS PIECES WITH HUMAN FIGURES.
PORTIONS OF WOOLLEN GARMENTS.
(Fig. 1 : 1/2; Figs. 2 and 3 : 1/3 of the natural size.)

Fig. 1. Nearly the whole surface is occupied by a figure drawn in straight lines. Portion of the upper part, the arms and head are preserved, and although the rest is destroyed, it may be partly restored from the outlines and separate remains. The body seems to have been clothed in a wide out-standing garment, leaving the feet and perhaps parts of the legs exposed. The arms, indicated by horizontal lines, stand out from the ornamented dress, the hands being turned at right angles upwards, while the fingers are suggested by four coloured squares. Each hand grasps a barbed hook turned towards the head. The large rectangular ears of the broad four-cornered head are attached to the blue face, to which the round red eyes and large mouth impart a grinning expression. The head-dress of the sitting figure in Fig. 2. of Plate 51. is recalled by two forked stripes projecting sidewards from the yellow band on the head.

This whimsical design is surrounded on three sides by a richly varied but badly preserved border interwoven in the material itself. Black step-shaped lines are traced in meandering figures round coloured spaces, in which the triangular form frequently recurs. These right-angled but not equilateral triangles, in which the hypothenuse is invariably composed of a step-edged line, form either alone or with other figures a frequently repeated motive in the designs of borders and materials, as in Fig. 1. of Plate 63.

2. The dress, from which this piece is taken, consisted of several portions corresponding exactly in size and design. Each is 39 centimetres broad and 11 high, a proportion so far noteworthy that the pieces were worked in these dimensions on the loom in such a way that the warp ran in the short direction.

The pattern consists of light and dark stripes with intervening bright lines. The ornament of the lighter stripes is formed of red and black heads on small stands, a red head corresponding to a black stand and vice versa. In this really childish drawing the mouth is beak-shaped while a light square represents the eye. In sewing the garment together no attention was paid to the arrangement of the several pieces, so that the heads stood sometimes erect sometimes reversed.

The dark stripes display a geometrical ornament with the colours tastefully disposed. To the lower hem of the garment are sewed yellow and red borders provided with short fringes.

3. Broad human features, each resting on three somewhat conical supports, and adorned with a large head-dress, constitute the frequently recurring ornament of the stripe, which is bordered by bands of simple design.

Fringed borders were not only applied to the lower hem of the garment, but were also sewed in between the stripes of the design.

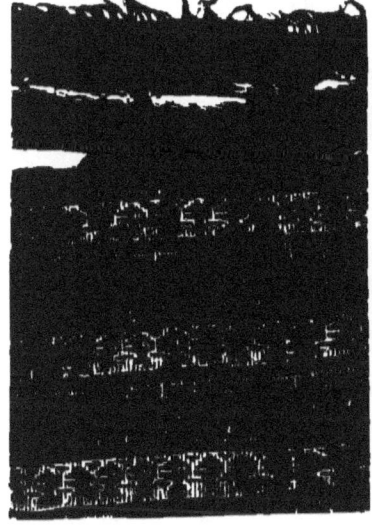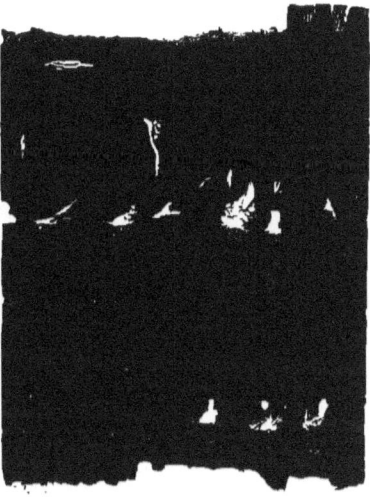

PLATE 53a.

FIGURED GOBELINS WITH GEOMETRICAL AND ANIMAL DESIGNS.
PORTIONS OF WOOLLEN GARMENTS.
(Natural size.)

Fig. 1. The large richly coloured specimen with geometrical figures seems strange amongst the other pieces ornamented mainly with animal and human figures. For although geometrical designs are not seldom used in dress materials, (see Plate 35, Figs. 1 and 2), they consist mostly of simple lines drawn in few colours. The peculiar crossing of the lines and figures suggests the character of the plaiting conditioned by the nature of the material employed.

As far as can be judged from the few preserved remnants, the garment was composed of narrow strips, one showing the pattern in horizontal, the other in vertical position. Two pointed heads on a kind of pedestal are introduced to fill up the corner spaces, which are enclosed by the truncated angles of the vertical compartments. The break in the slits peculiar to gobelins work is avoided by interweaving threads of the bordering colours in the warp of the neighbouring colours.

2. Small gobelins piece with interwoven woollen border. The preserved portion is divided into nearly square fields serving as spaces for conventional animal figures. The colours both of the grounds and figures vary. The rows of fields are separated on both sides by meandering step lines, which are also introduced vertically between the several fields, thus developing a complete frame, the various parts of which seem to be very aptly connected together. This animal figure frequently recurs as a motive in the ornamentation both of woven fabrics and earthenware. Body, legs and tail are given in profile, but the head in full view, so that the animal appears to be looking round to the spectator. Of the legs two only are visible, as if the two others were concealed by them.

The coloured border stripes are not woven in the Gobelins style, but the pattern is produced by throwing the coloured woof at regular intervals across several threads in the warp.

3. This fragment is distinguished by the number (some 7 or 8) and variety of the patterns here crowded into a narrow space. Of large bird figures there remain only the legs and tail feathers. Smaller birds are introduced in ascending rows on oblique vandyked strips. A short horizontal band shows the frequently recurring motive apparently of conventional bird figures interlaced with each other, while the many-coloured and diversely partitioned fields of the lower portion are adorned with four smaller ornaments. Here specially noteworthy are the white crosses or clover designs in the brown corner, as well as the double-beaked figures half red half brown.

PLATE 54.

DRESS MATERIALS WITH GEOMETRICAL PATTERNS.

(Figs. 1 and 2 = ⅕; Figs. 3 and 4 = ½ of the natural size.)

The four woollen pieces are worked in the Gobelins manner. Three consist of narrow stripes separately woven and connected by seams, while in the fourth (Fig. 2) the ornamental stripes are woven into the material.

Fig. 1. Dress material composed of borders and striped pieces. Red, yellow and white patterns about 7½ centimeters wide are enclosed on either side by narrow red borders, and the whole garment is made up of the tripartite bands thus produced. Between the broad stripes are thus inserted narrow borders in twoes; but at the lower end there is one such border only, to which is sewed the edge consisting of yellow and black indented triangles with fringe attached. The broad stripes have a flat pattern, whose design becomes intelligible by placing two of the corresponding stripes in juxta-position. It consists of Ϝ-shaped yellow brown figures in contact and disposed in vertical rows one above the other. A second row of the same figures in red, and reversed, is displaced half a figure's length towards the first, both dovetailing in such a way that the extremities of the Ϝ Ϝ touch each other. The red Ϝ is yellow inside, while the yellow brown is bordered in white. In this specimen the ornamented design is most effective on the white coloured stripes. These rows, pressed close together in like position, are repeated with uniform disposition of the colours, but of course touch only at the projecting angles, thus leaving between them rows of diagonally disposed squares. These squares are filled in with the colours of the pattern, the horizontal rows always consisting of uniformly coloured squares, while squares bordered alternately in yellow and red follow successively from top to bottom. A peculiar effect is imparted to the whole design by the fact that all the coloured bands consist of small squares in contact only at the corners. — In the narrow borders appropriate light and dark red bird figures are so interlocked as to fill up the whole space. This design has been obviously evolved from a simple Meander, whose lines have by slight changes been transformed to the contour of the bird figures.

2. Dress material with meandering stripes. At a right angle to the warp run stripes of like width and design, but differently coloured. By means of a meandering line each stripe is disposed in two equal parts, which, being differently coloured, form the interlocked hook pattern. The side border shows the same design, but with greater variety of colours and partly more irregularly executed.

3. Dress material composed of narrow borders. Each border is formed of two rows of congruent equilateral triangles, which are so fitted one into the other that the teeth of the sides running obliquely with the warp are closely interlocked. The triangles in one row of each border are of like colour, whereas those of the other rows are alternately of two different colours. The several borders are so stitched together that the bases of the differently coloured triangles always meet. Some of the seams appear to betray signs of rude and hasty mendings.

4. Coarse dress material with the simplest meandering ornamentation. The pattern of the stripes, about 7 centimeters broad, is formed of two-coloured bands, ascending and descending in the simplest meandering style. The two portions divided by these lines are diversely coloured, showing irregular dispositions of the colours in the series of stripes.

PLATE 55.

GOBELINS STUFFS WITH GEOMETRICAL PATTERNS AND ANIMAL FIGURES.
PARTS OF WOOLLEN GARMENTS.
(Fig. 1 — ¹/₁; Figs. 2 and 3 — ¹/₄ of the natural size.)

Fig. 1. The large pattern with its simple divisions and the prevailing gray ground tone of the whole colouring imparts to this piece an effect deviating from that of other Ancon woven fabrics. In the light gray ground are inserted squares with wide black stripes, which are disposed in diagonal rows in such a way that the successive rows appear as if displaced towards each other half a diameter's length of the figures. The square rows are kept so far apart as to leave between them zig-zag stripes of the ground colour of the same width as the black bands enclosing the squares. The zig-zag lines are connected by short gray stripes, which cut off the corners of the squares placed in a row. This simple design is further set off either by bird-figures so disposed in the gray stripes between the black-enframed squares that they seem to be moving on both sides from the upper corners of the squares downwards, or else by a number of ornaments reserved in the black frame of the large squares, or lastly by a large design in the centre of these squares. As a reserved pattern, the form of the square, with the corners cut off right and left, is repeated eighteen times in each of the black frames on a reduced scale and in a somewhat distorted fashion. A small ring-shaped ornament very irregularly executed occupies the interior of this square. The central figure of the large squares faintly preserved in blue and red is a far from rare form (see Plate 53a, Fig. 1 and Plate 66, Figs. 5—6), symmetrically developped above and below, right and left, and apparently reducible to a wicker-work motive.

In the execution of the design much irregularity is shown both in the drawing of the several ornaments and in the often arbitrarily modified colouring. Thus the small ornament repeated eighteen times in the light figures reserved in the black frames of the squares appears here as two concentric rings, there as spirals, elsewhere as a rectangle with a straight stroke in the centre, once even merely as a crooked line. Equally irregular are the bird-figures, of which one especially, above to the left, appears simply as a brown speck.

2. The fabric is crossed transversely by simple zig-zag stripes closely united. Five different colours between yellow, brown and black are repeated in regular sequence. The piece terminates below with a meandering border woven on, whose surface is filled in with colours like those of the pattern above.

3. The garment was made up of narrow stripes in the same way as those figured on Plate 54, Figs. 1, 3 and 4. Each stripe consists of a wide central part bordered above and below by a narrow red edging. To the lower stripe are further woven broad yellow tabs as a fringe stitched together, as is frequently the case. Possibly this was done to prevent the fringes from rolling up. In the black stripes is repeated a yellow design bordered by step-lines, consisting of regularly disposed groups, each of which may be regarded as formed of four highly conventionalised human figures joined at the feet.

PLATE 55a.

DRESS MATERIALS AND BORDERINGS.

Figs. 1–5; 1–6; Fig. 6 = F.1 of the natural size.

Fig. 1. Wide woollen bordering with pattern somewhat indistinctly defined owing to the method of weaving adopted. The black ground of the ornamented portion is crossed by obliquely disposed meandering stripes. By means of inserted heads and vandyked lines the meanders have been converted into a bird ornament executed in alternate yellow and red colours. The piece is finished off on one side with narrow brown stripes threaded together in the simplest way.

2. Brown cotton material with interwoven woollen Gobelins borders. The brightly ornamented stripes lie close to the hem. From the woollen ground stand out black-edged figures treated as faces, disposed in two rows, and executed in diverse colours. In both rows of each border the same figure is constantly repeated, reversed in the lower row and displaced by half the diameter of the figure. By means of narrow zig-zag bands each figure of one row is connected with the two above it of the other row, thus producing a continuous ornament ascending and descending in broken lines.

3. Narrow woollen border, obliquely intersected breadthwise by the coloured stripes. Here yellow stripes with inserted red fish figures alternate with red stripes, in which thin heads terminating with hooks serve as an ornament. Between these stripes are introduced yellow and red vandyked bands.

4. The narrow woollen Gobelins border, which had apparently been woven to a larger piece, displays between black and yellow parallel stripes a simple motive repeatedly recurring and consisting of an elliptical head with four horn-like hooks attached.

5. Woollen Gobelins piece. Regular yellow and red hexagons are disposed in parallel rows, the red being connected together by narrow stripes, so that the yellow surfaces appear as if designed on a red ground. The same motive executed in black recurs in all the hexagons.

6. Piece of a large woollen poncho resembling Figs. 2 and 4 of Plate 35. The yellow ground is crossed by red stripes finished off below in step-like lines, and leaving intervening wide yellow bands. Into the latter has been introduced an animal ornament consisting of long-eared heads, which terminate below in two hook-shaped lines. These recur throughout the whole length of the poncho grouped one above another in black and red couples. In each stripe the heads of like colour stand on the same side above each other, but alternate in the several stripes. A twofold alternation is also shown in the arrangement of the colours, the design appearing in one pair dark on a yellow ground, in the next yellow on a dark ground. The ornamental stripes are edged on both sides with narrow borders consisting of zig-zag lines and inserted rhombs. To the red heads is attached a black, to the black a red border.

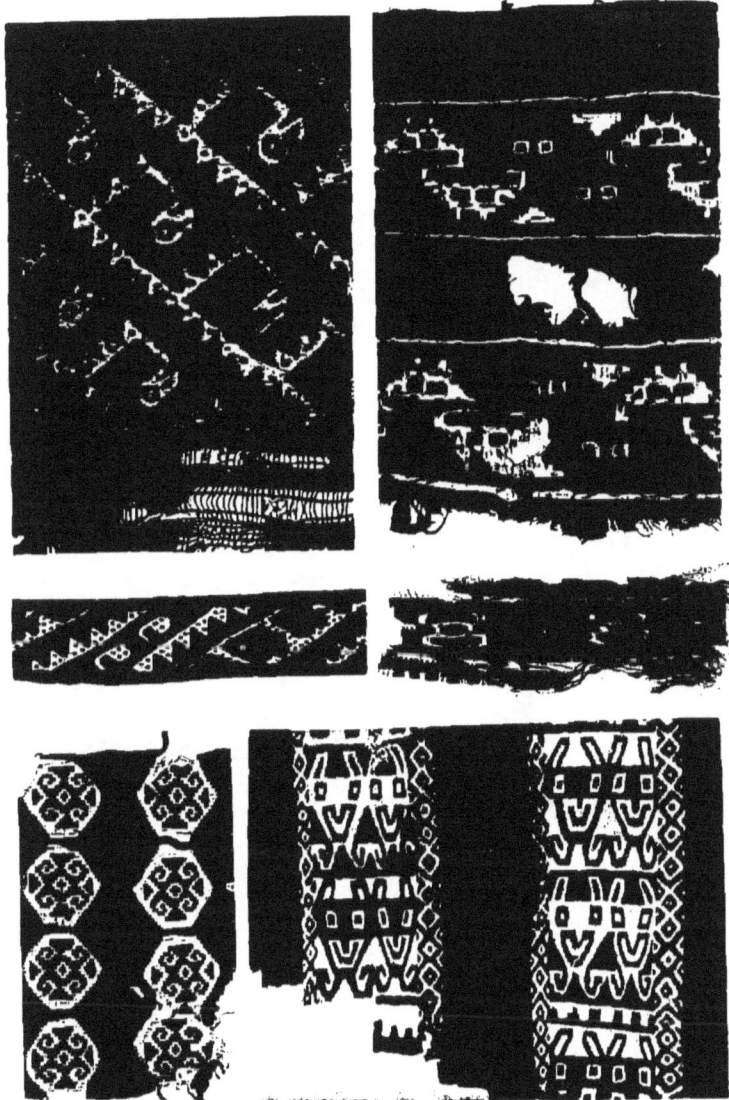

PLATE 56.

WOOLLEN GOBELINS FABRICS WITH ANIMAL FIGURES.

(Figs. 1 and 2 natural size; Fig. 3 = ⅓ of the natural size.)

Fig. 1. Narrow strips of a thick Gobelins material with both sides bordered in red. The pattern consists of red and yellow stripes disposed in large zig-zag lines lengthwise, always intersecting the warp at an oblique angle. These stripes, about 1½ centimeter broad, are grouped in couples divided by a narrow band in alternating colours and with one of its edges vandyked. Within the broad stripes animal figures are so disposed that they seem to be descending in procession on either side down the slopes from the salient corners of the zig-zag lines. In the inner angles of these lines the figures consequently meet full butt, while at the projecting corners they are turned in twos back to back. The latter disposition is skilfully utilised to connect two figures together, and even the free space in the upper corner is appropriately occupied by a floating figure. Although executed in a very rude manner these animals are shown from their curly tails to be quadrupeds. The eye is suggested in the head by a mark exactly like another introduced in the middle of the body. The several parts of the pattern are edged in black, while the uniformity of the ground is broken by light and dark spots suitably disposed. The purpose of the fabric can scarcely be determined from the scraps that have been preserved. It may have served either for a pouch, or in combination with other strips may have been worked up into a garment.

2. Narrow border-like woven strips, with the warp running obliquely, and the whole coarsely sewed together in a single piece. The ornament belongs to the already oft-mentioned type, in which the pattern is made up of two harmonising portions so interlocked as completely to fill the whole space. Here we have two alternate rows of conventional heads (Plate 55 a) connected together by narrow bands. The red-edged pattern is rendered more effective by the diverse shadings of the surface.

3. Portion of a gorgeously coloured Gobelins fabric, which was deposited in an unfinished state in the grave with the dead. This is obvious both from the outer parts left unclosed, and from the ends of the coloured threads still attached to the reverse side. The material is of rich design and colour, and is partly exceedingly well preserved. The pattern departs perceptibly from the regularity by which most of the Ancon woven fabrics are distinguished. In some of the stripes, notably those to the right of the observer, the wave and vandyked lines are correctly executed, while a keen sense of nature is betrayed in the bird-figures, in whose crest, hooked beak and broad tail we clearly recognise the Condor. But towards the left the wave lines merge in detached rows of circles and ellipses; the serrated lines are changed to irregular scallopings, and the condor is replaced by ill-shaped animals mostly without crest and with the beak even reversed to the breast. It would seem as if a weaver less skilled at drawing had attempted symmetrically to repeat on the left the pattern begun on the right side. The distorted figures would thus be explained by the difficulties associated with such copying.

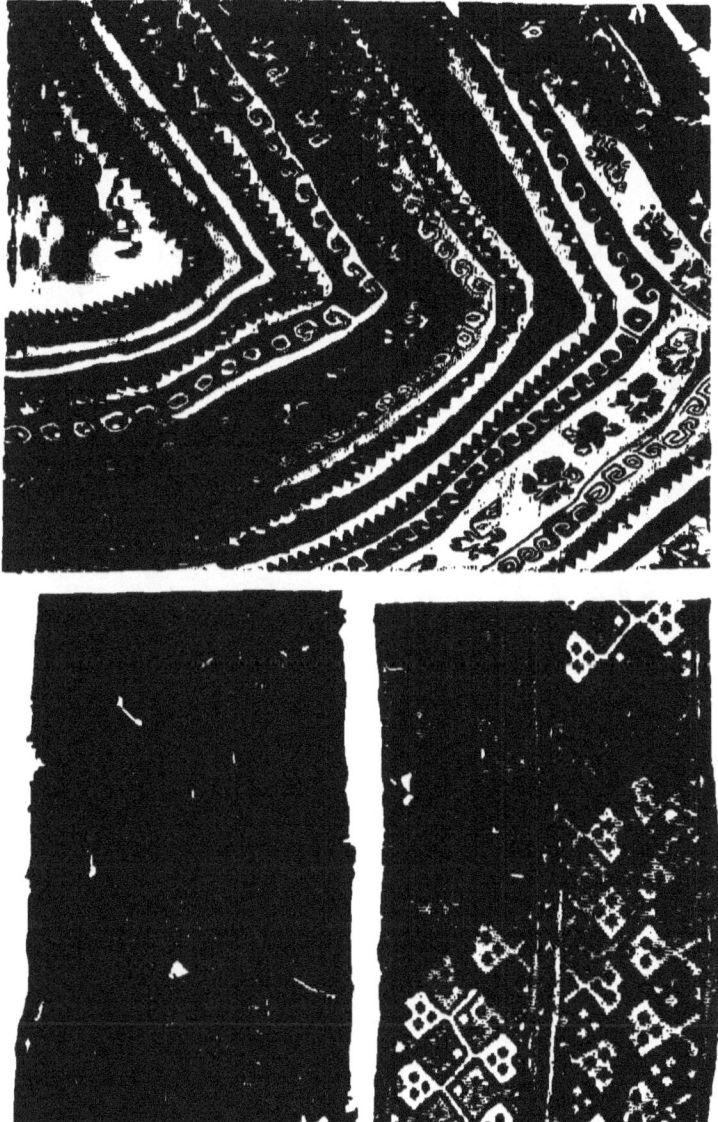

PLATE 57.

BOLDLY ORNAMENTED DRESS MATERIALS.

(Fig. 1 = ⅛; Fig. 2 = ¼ of the natural size.)

Although richly ornamented fabrics were almost exclusively woven in the Gobelins method, it is evident from a number of garments and borders with variegated patterns that great skill had already been acquired in more intricate styles. Such are the two specimens here figured, which are especially noteworthy for their bold designs.

Fig. 1. A cotton fabric with interwoven woollen ornaments; the ground being formed of a thick cotton material with yellow, grey and brown stripes obliquely intersected by a large meandering and hooked pattern. This design constantly repeated forms a broad band limited above and below by narrow woollen borders traversed by thin cotton stripes. The several sections of the oblique band are gradually reduced in size upwards, so that the third or topmost is scarcely half as large as the lowest. This woollen design is carried out in red and yellow alternate lines running diagonally athwart the whole pattern. In the preparation of this peculiar fabric, in which the cross-weaving of the ornamental part differs from that of the ground, the woollen design was first woven, and the intervening spaces afterwards filled in with the coloured cotton stripes. Hence the slits at the edges; hence also the peculiarity that the cotton stripes do not run uniformly, or recur in the same sequence in the different ground compartments.

2. A woollen piece, in which the diagonal disposition of the yarn produces a sort of twilled material. The thin brown and somewhat coarse texture is disposed in large spaces by green strips some 13 centimeters broad, in which, by reserving space for the brown, the design is produced of a face decorated with spiral appendages. On the wrong side the disposition of the colours is reversed, here the design being in green on a brown ground. In the ornamented strips alone both green and brown are jointly introduced, the ground threads here always showing through sufficiently to tone the sharp contrast of both colours.

PLATE 58.

ORNAMENTAL COTTON GARMENT WITH WOOLLEN BORDER.
(⅓ of the natural size.)

Of the garment, of which this fragment formed part, a few portions only have been found in good condition. It consists of an unusually fine and thick white cotton fabric ornamented with bright-coloured wool in such a way that the raised pattern resembles embroidery. The lower end, a sort of richly ornamented edging, is formed by a woollen border woven on to the cotton material and provided with a fringe.

The woollen design consists of indented triangles in red, yellow and violet-brown, so disposed as to form vertical rows. In each row the triangles are uniformly disposed, but in the several rows the indented side faces upwards and downwards alternately. In the arrangement of the various triangles within the vertical rows a certain regularity may be detected, those of like colour running together in diagonal lines, whereby the whole surface becomes disposed in large squares. Each side of such a square is composed of six red triangles; the centre is occupied by four violet-brown triangles the intervening space being assigned to the rows of yellow triangles. This arrangement may be clearly seen in the left portion of the illustration. The corner to the right, which is here out of place, is introduced for the sake of the general effect. Each of the coloured triangles is divided into rhombic figures, with the inner space filled in with an animal face (Plate 58a).

The border is woven directly on to the garment, several of the thin cotton threads being united to form one thick thread in the warp of the woollen fabric and carried right through to the extremities of the fringe. The Gobelins border itself consists of a broad central strip bounded by two narrow bands which are disposed in different colours. On the yellow ground of the central strip an animal ornament in red outline is introduced similar to that in Fig. 2 of Plate 56, showing the frequent recurrence of a quadruped's and bird's head alternately. The design runs transversely to the direction of the border, and each of its elements is made up of four animal heads, of which the two to the right as well as those to the left are severally connected in a single group by means of long neck-like stripes. Between these groups the birds' heads are inserted. The same element, so alternated one with the other as to fill up the whole space, is repeated above and below, to the right and left with absolute uniformity. The pattern would be more distinct had the several spaces been coloured differently, whereas as it is we seem to detect on the uniform yellow ground nothing but a confused maze of red lines. The pattern may in the simplest manner be reduced to six rows of diagonally disposed squares.

In the narrow side bands there is introduced an ornament in bright yellow, apparently intended as a fish. The broad and very peculiar tabs of the fringe betray a regular disposition of colours, each group of five yellow tabs being separated by a triple system of red, yellow and brown ones.

PLATE 59.

DRESS MATERIALS HORIZONTALLY STRIPED.

(Fig. 1 full size; Fig. 2. ⅔ of the natural size.)

Fig. 1. Horizontal stripes of a pattern executed in wool are interwoven in a thin cotton material. The garment, from which this fragment is taken, was trimmed with a broad yellow-fringed border. The woollen stripes consist of yellow and red worsted so interwoven that the design, red on the right, appears yellow on the wrong side, as shown in the two halves of the illustration. The two lower stripes show one side, the four upper the other side of the fabric. The design represents a constantly recurring series of fully schematized animal heads connected in pairs by zig-zag lines.

The woven border displays an exactly similar motive, more richly carried out. Here the fringes are sewed on.

2. Piece of a woollen garment. Yellow and red stripes cross each other horizontally; but the latter show merely a simple rep-like structure, whereas the former are covered with fine ornamental work. On a light yellow ground is raised a seemingly confused mass of tangled lines, which however on a closer inspection become disposed in definite ornamental designs. The same pattern prevails as in Fig. 1, where it stands out more clearly, and may be more easily understood. The fabric is provided with a wide border, into the dark ground of which an animal motive is interwoven. A bird, with body and wings by means of inserted lozenge-shaped figures changed to a dog or a lion's face, is repeated in several rows in upright and reversed attitudes. The birds themselves are connected together by means of serrated diagonal lines. The outer hem of the border is adorned with broad fringe-like stripes.

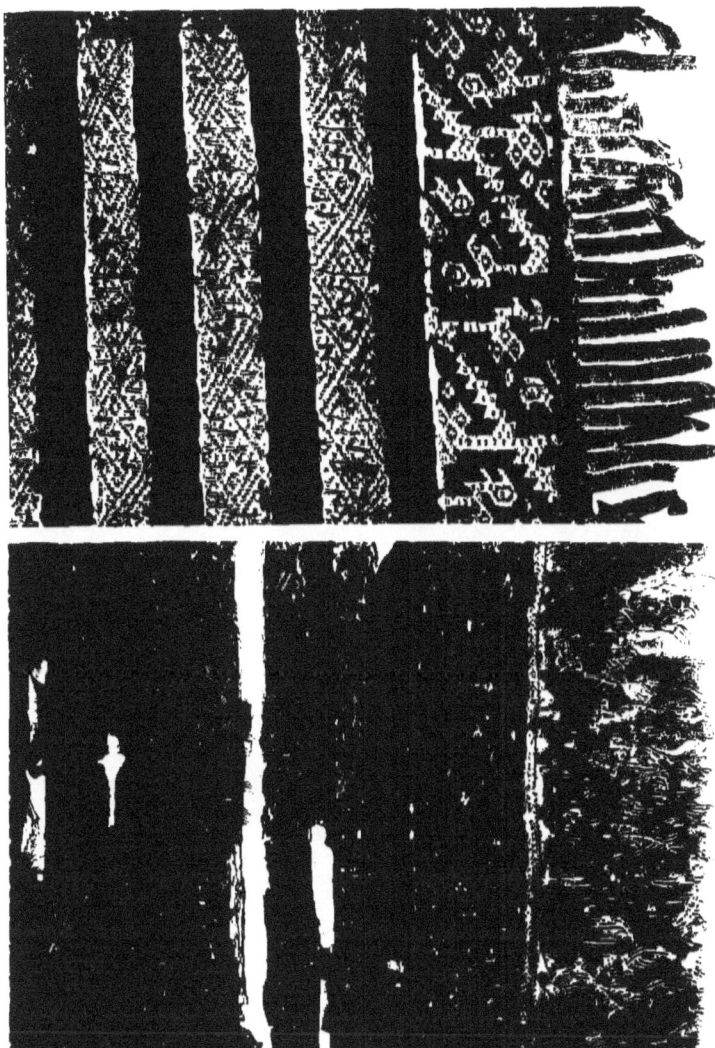

PLATE 59a.

COTTON DRESS MATERIALS.

Figs. 1—3 (?) Fig. 4 = 1/2 of the natural size.

Fig. 1. To the plain coloured piece is woven an ornamental cotton border, whose design closely matching it in colour produces a quiet harmonious effect. It consists of the frequently recurring obliquely disposed meandering stripes, both of whose flat elements are kept in diverse shades of brown, while the intervening meander-line itself is formed by spots of some bright thread. The meander displays those manifold scallopings characteristic of the transition to the bird ornament. This central portion of the border is edged by two narrow stripes, in which quite a peculiar embellishment is attained by diversely shading the several sections of the same meander motive. From the rest of the material the whole border is distinguished as well by its looser texture as by the design itself.

2. Regularly disposed systems of bright stripes intersect the dark material, whose edge is adorned by two interwoven narrow woollen borders standing somewhat apart from each other. A meander-line of the simplest kind divides each of the woollen borders into two parts, of which the upper exhibits a yellow, the lower a brown colour.

3. Brown cotton stuff woven with great uniformity, and crossed by wide bright and narrow dark stripes. By way of ornament dark brown cotton threads are so interwoven that, while forming a regular pattern, they appear to be braided on. This pattern consists of cruciform figures enclosed by step-like lines ascending and descending and running at right angles to the coloured stripes.

4. Light dress material embellished near the edge with bright interwoven borders. Here the lower portion alone is figured. A like pattern is displayed by both borders, which are edged by narrow brown stripes and separated by an intervening stripe of the simple cotton material. The border is intersected breadthwise by obliquely disposed meandering stripes modified to a bird motive. The white bordering lines are reserved between the woollen threads by which the design is effected. But the bright details are so faded that the colours can scarcely be any longer recognised. Only in the bird's head, here very characteristically designed, the red orbit of the eye, the yellow pupil and the yellow beak are sharply defined. The hem is at once strengthened and adorned with an elegant design by reversing the material.

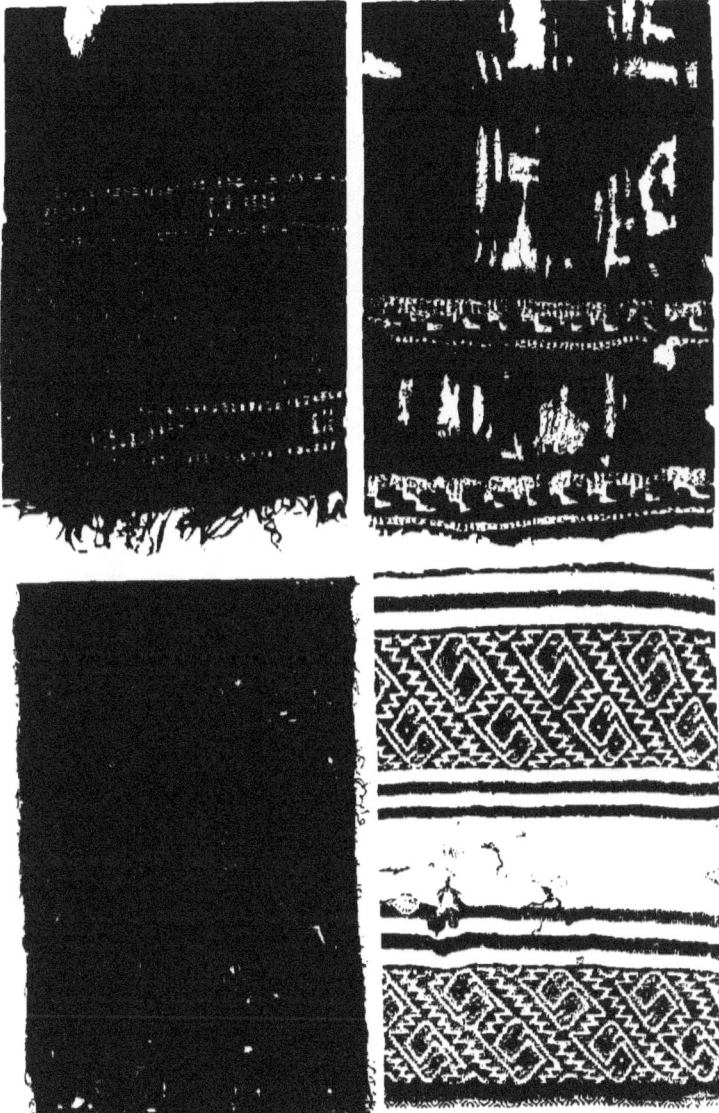

PLATE 60.

DRESS MATERIALS WITH PASSEMENTERIE TRIMMINGS.

(⅔ of the natural size.)

In a certain class of sumptuous garments a thin gauze-like cotton fabric forms the foundation for diverse passementerie adornments raised in rich colours on the transparent ground. They are mostly narrow, simply ornamented borders sewed in regular order to the light material, and thus imparting to it greater firmness. They serve as supports for braid and rosettes worked in relief with bright tassels and fringes. Garments put together in this way must have been very destructible, the ornaments falling apart, when the flimsy cotton fabric decayed. Hence the very fragmentary pieces here reproduced rather suggest the sumptuous character of such garments than convey any real picture of their appearance.

Fig. 1. The gauze-like foundation has still been partly preserved, thereby showing the disposition of the borders. Narrow, reps-like stripes of a yellow-red woollen fabric are sewed at regular intervals to the cotton material. The vertical rows traverse the entire dress, while the two horizontal stripes form the lower edge, consequently serve to some extent as borders. To each stripe are attached narrow, red strings, two running parallel with the edges, while two other undulating lines intersecting each other entwine the blue crosses interwoven in the yellow-red ground. The borders thus adorned are further superabundantly supplied with elegant red tassels. The space between the stripes is also filled with passementerie work, so that the foundation is almost completely hidden. Two essentially different motives here alternate: first a narrow green braid with dark red rosettes from the centre of which fall several interlaced bundles of tassels; then thin red braids grouped in a ladder pattern and connected with a narrow fringed border, which also bears a number of tassels.

2. The ground has entirely disappeared, so that the disposition of the several parts is doubtful. In the vertical stripes figures are interwoven, whose narrow, band-like bodies support large heads. Hands and feet as well as the tips of the long winding tails and of the large outstanding ears serve somewhat comically to suspend small tassels which swing with every movement. Although the faces are almost human, the form of the whole head rather recalls the animal figured on Plate 53a, Fig. 2, and Plate 64, Fig. 2, and frequently recurring elsewhere. The trimming of this garment consisted of a broad stripe composed of several borders with a fine meandering design.

3. Amongst the decayed remnants of the dress a few only of the trimmings were well preserved. Large rosettes are attached to a double row of braid adorned with small tassels. Each rosette consists of narrow strings disposed concentrically which, corresponding to the warp of a textile fabric, served as the inlay for the red woollen threads used in the overspinning. The edge of the rosette is bordered by a fringed hem, while a number of yellow and black strings (11—13) ending at the periphery in red tassels, radiate from the centre, which is indicated by a blue ring, and which also serves as an attachment for a large bundle of tassels. The large tassels in this piece, as well as in Fig. 1 generally consist of a thick tuft of short light red wool, with the long dark red threads starting from the centre.

PLATE 60a.

PASSEMENTERIE WORK.

Fig. 1 – 4: Figs. 2, 3, 5 ⅓ of the natural size.

To the rich gauze-like garments with inserted passementerie work, a few examples of which were given on the previous Plate, belong also those articles of dress to the transparently woven ground material of which were sewed ornaments of a firm Gobelins type. Of other passementerie work there frequently occurred rosettes adorned with tufts and tassels, which were apparently fastened to garments, and to head or neck-bands. A long narrow article of attire prepared quite in this style has already been figured on Plate 43, Fig. 8.

Fig. 1. Gobelins ornament from a gauze-like garment. The design, mostly executed in various shades of yellow, stands out on the red ground of the somewhat irregularly fashioned piece. It represents a recumbent human figure with large head-dress disproportionately expanded by the attached borders. On a light yellow couch lies the figure clothed in a kind of shirt, the legs represented one above the other, one in fact suspended in the air. One arm alone is visible, its hand raising to the open mouth some article of a bracket type with a large object visible at one end. Both garment and legs are ornamented, and the ankles and three toes of the feet are indicated. A collar encircles the bare neck, and the hat-shaped head-gear is fashioned like that figured on Plate 51, Fig. 1. To the lower edge of the Gobelins material are fastened loose dangling fringes.

2. Trimming of the flowing robe figured on Plate 43, Fig. 8. Here is reproduced on a larger scale one of the pieces of trimming attached to the lower end of the long stripe decorated with rich passementerie work. A square Gobelins-piece is edged on three sides by a border adorned with bright oblique stripes radiating from the central portion. To the lower edge of the main piece thus fashioned is applied a broad red border concealing the appended long twisted fringes. Each of these fringes bears at its lower end a smooth red tassel, and the small Gobelins-piece is embellished with a human figure exactly like that described in Fig. 4.

3. Trimming like Fig. 2. Around three sides of a nearly square Gobelins-piece are applied and firmly sewed first two narrow red, then a wider brightly striped border. To the third side thus widened long fringes had been fastened, of which only a few remnants survive. On the red ground of the Gobelins-piece a human figure with large head-dress is represented, its legs disposed sideways in order to make room for the suspended ends of the waist-band.

4. Trimming formed of a red Gobelins stripe of somewhat rectangular shape and encircled by an obliquely striped border. In the Gobelins-piece itself are interwoven two conventional human figures, whose feet are turned toward each other, and both of whom are decked with a large widely extended head-gear.

5. Rosette-shaped trimming. A spherical surface edged with a many-coloured border represents a human figure, whose upper portion is encircled by a wreath of short diverse coloured fringes. To the lower side are attached long red woollen fringes ending in yellow tassels. The central fringes are somewhat longer than those on either side.

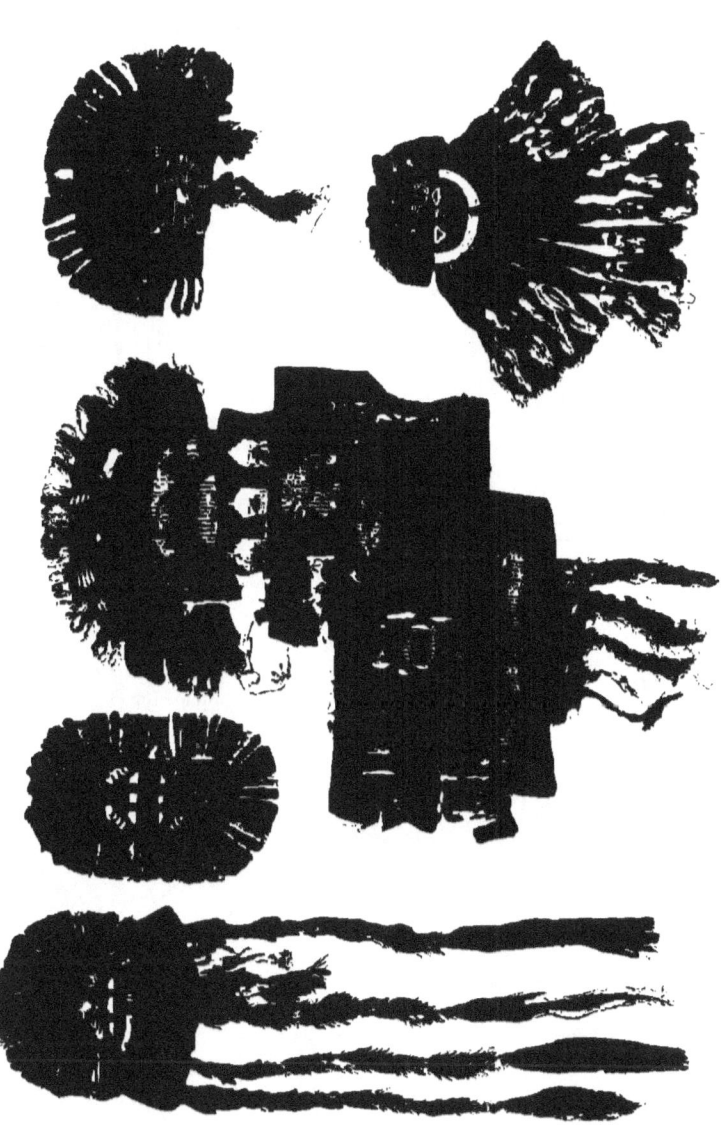

PLATE 61.

BORDER OF A ROBE OF THE TALARIA TYPE.
(Natural size.)

The illustrations on plates 41—3, and especially the last, give the general form of the garments, of which the present is merely the upper border.

Peculiar to the border seems to be the angular scalloping, which here also occurs in the middle piece. All the parallel stripes meet together at the same angle, their meandering design running on both sides from the edge to the centre, so that the whole piece seems as if it were formed of two symmetrical halves.

The borders round the middle piece, whose projecting ends represent faces, are woven separately and carefully sewed on with the needle. However geometrically disposed the interwoven design may seem to be, it none the less suggests human faces, as we may easily convince ourselves by fixing our attention on the part of the figure which remains exposed after concealing a third portion above or below. In the faces adorning the semi-circular projecting ends of the side borders the eyes and teeth alone are clearly indicated, the nose being merely suggested by two cross strokes. The yellow fringes are sewed on, but the narrow red braiding is embroidered on the fabric in the tambour style.

The symmetry of the highly coloured design is relieved of its pedantic formality by many little arbitrary touches in the execution, and although eight different colours are disposed side by side the whole produces a harmonious effect.

The unornamented robes illustrated on plates 41—2 were found almost exclusively in the graves of that part of the Necropolis which is indicated by figure 9 on the plan, whereas remnants of the borderings were amongst the most frequent finds in all the graves.

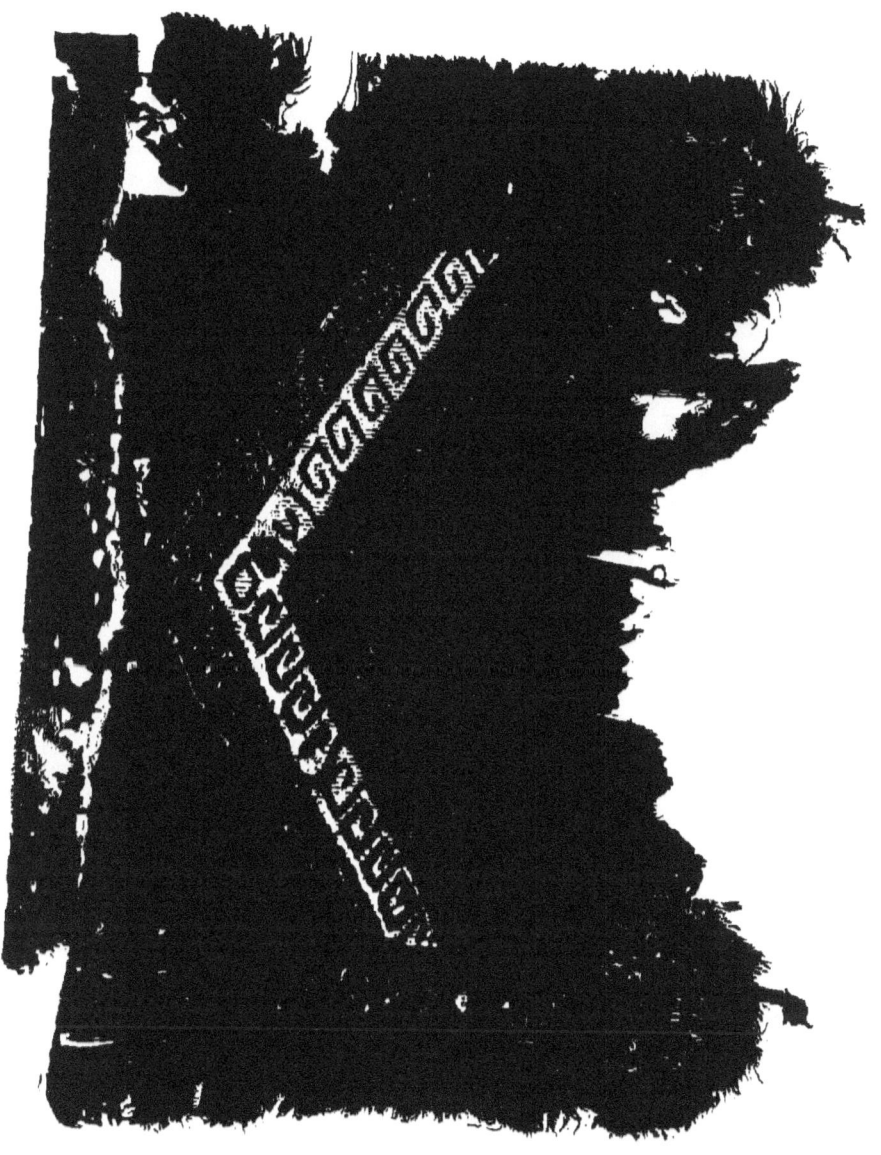

PLATE 62.

WOOLLEN BORDER OF A FLOWING GARMENT.

(Natural size.)

This is the border of the garment figured on Plate 43, Fig. 6, but is here reversed and reproduced in its natural size. The thick woollen fabric woven in the Gobelins style is disposed in three strips, two yellow and one red, and is hemmed over at both ends. In the illustration it merges upwards in broad band-like fringes, the meandering pattern of which betrays great irregularity. The lower hem has been stiffened or padded by being faced with a border embellished with many-coloured waving lines.

In the three broad strips the only ornament is a human figure constantly recurring in a series of rows. These figures with their black contours are drawn with long neck and rudely outlined head, in which the bright circle, probably representing an eye, is the only suggestion of the features. Body and arms are envelopped in a garment of rectangular form, whose bright pattern is scrupulously suggested. Below it are shown the claw-footed legs. Notwithstanding the defective and childish drawing of the human figure, a good ornamental effect is produced by the general disposition. This is still better seen in the whole piece, as figured on Plate 43, Fig. 6.

It gives the impression that this portion was originally woven for some other purpose and afterwards made to do duty as the border of a flowing garment. At least this would seem to be implied by the fringes firmly sewed to the cotton fabric and thus rendered useless, as well as by the circumstance that, as now applied, the human figures are made to stand on their head.

PLATE 62a.

TRIMMINGS OF ROBES OF THE TALARIA TYPE.
WOOLLEN MATERIALS.

Figs. 1—4., 7.: Figs. 5, 6.: ⅓, of the natural size.

The upper trimmings of these long-flowing garments consist usually of three parts — a broad central piece edged right and left by two borders. Each of these pieces is often separately prepared, but the borders are also often woven on to the middle piece. Of both kinds examples are here given in supplement to Plates 41—45, 61—63. Most of the side borders show at their lower end, which projects beyond the bright central piece, a rounded off and fringed attachment embellished with a highly conventionalised human face.

Fig. 1. Side border, by red and yellow horizontal stripes disposed in three superimposed sections. In all three is repeated the same pattern of red-edged rhombes placed close together, and enclosing three red crosses. The upper halves of each diamond-shaped figure are uniformly yellow, while the lower halves are diversely coloured. The limit between both colours attaches itself to the enclosed crosses, thus producing a pleasant colour-pattern.

2. Side border. The pattern consists of variously coloured zig-zag stripes running obliquely across the border, and separated from each other by stripes of the yellow ground. In the middle of the border run two violet stripes, while at both ends appear blue-green stripes in twoes. The whole coloured design is crossed by two systems of parallel lines which, intersecting each other at an acute angle, dispose the piece in small, red-edged rhombes. The border was not woven on the loom, but worked in a kind of chain-stitch, or perhaps with a crochet-needle.

3. Side border in Gobelins work. The pattern is formed of obliquely-disposed meander-stripes, merging in an animal ornament. The adjoining surfaces of every two neighbouring meander-bands are of like colour, giving the impression that the inter-locked design is formed by the repetition of a narrow stem with hook-formed appendages branching off on either side. The several sections of the design have coloured edgings.

4. Narrow Gobelins border with fringed appendage. The design shows animal figures alternately black on a red and red on a black ground. From the intervening ornamentation it would appear that this is a section of some larger surface pattern.

5. Part of a trimming with side border woven on. The border shows alternating black and yellow stripes, into which a meander passing into an animal motive has been worked in red thread. In the broad middle piece the yellow ground is adorned with rhombes disposed in rows, and in which the double figure of a bird is reserved. Between the rhombes are regularly disposed red dotted lines.

6. Central portion of a trimming, corresponding in texture and design with the foregoing, except that here in the dark rhombes yellow squares, instead of bird figures, are reserved.

7. Central portion of a trimming woven in the same way as Figs. 5 and 6. The design is a variation of the ornament already shown in Plate 55a, Fig. 2. The woollen material is finished off with a wide hem embellished with a pretty meandering stripe.

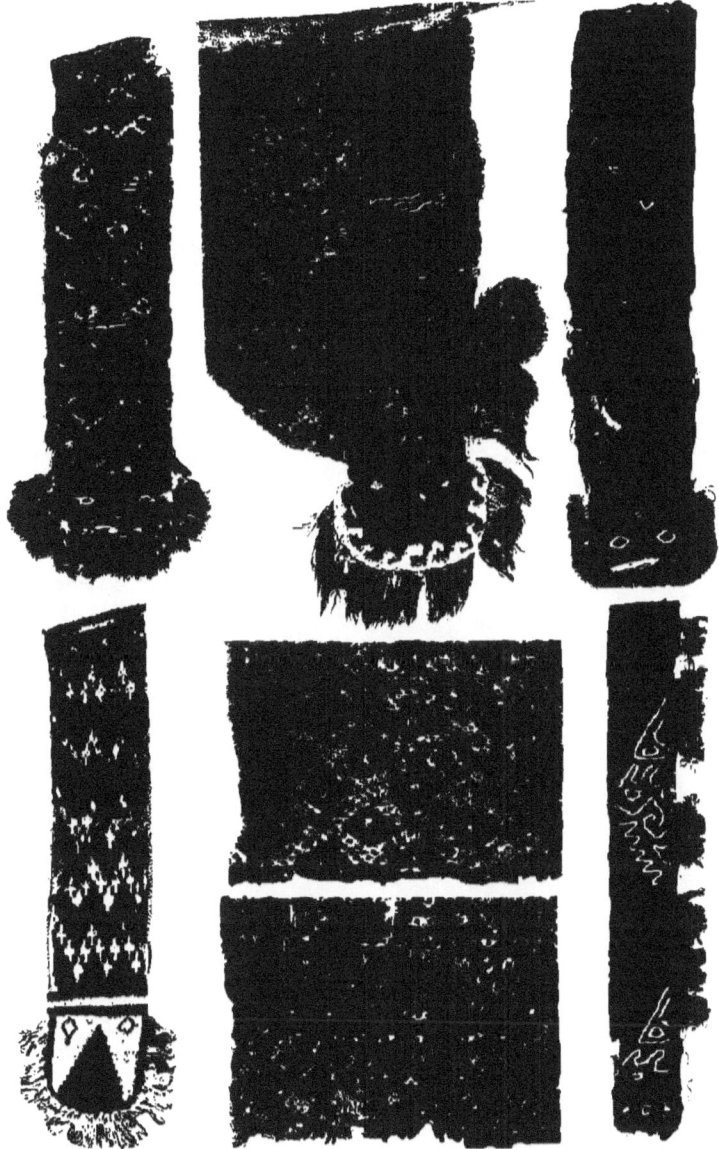

PLATE 63.

(Figs. 1—4 natural size.)

I. BORDERS OF FLOWING GARMENTS.

Fig. 1. Closely woven woollen Gobelins fabric, 9 centim. long and 26 broad, completely enclosed on all four sides, intended apparently as the border of a flowing garment. The upper and lower edging of this richly figured piece is formed by meandering strips, the former broad and many-coloured, the latter narrow and dark-coloured. The intervening space is divided by two parallel red lines into two strips of about the same depth. In the upper strip a peculiar ornament is repeated in two consecutive rows. Two differently coloured triangular figures are reversed towards each other in such a way that their serrated hypothenuses dovetail although still separated by a narrow stripe of the yellow ground. The broad portion of the triangles shows a bright or dark enframed square like an eye, imparting to the whole the appearance of a distorted face. A short line projecting from the lower end of the triangles to the left terminates with a shorter vertical line, which serves to support a bird of the same colour as the respective triangle. It is noteworthy that the ornament of the serrated triangles is also introduced in the upper edge into the spaces enclosed in the blue meandering lines.

The lower section is again divided into two strips ornamented with birds of a very simple type, and with the motive of the upper portion irregularly repeated.

2. Details of the border, Plate 43, Fig. 5. The Gobelins fabric is distinguished by the beauty of its colours, its delicate woollen yarn, uniformity of texture and correct drawing. Red and yellow strips vandyked and dovetailed into each other intersect the warp at an angle of about 45°, running parallel with the lower edge of the border. Within the strips are figures resembling the heraldic two-headed eagles, bordered in red or black, and executed in diverse colours.

II. ORNAMENTED WOOLLEN CORNER PIECES.

Cotton garments and cloths of diverse use often display richly ornamented corners mostly interwoven with bright wool in the Gobelins manner.

3. The bright woollen corner-piece is woven into the white cotton fabric, several threads of the thin material being united to form the thread of the warp. As oblique lines in weaving appear broken, the step-like borders have here been executed on a larger scale and made to serve as an ornament, whereby on the edges running parallel with the warp fissures are naturally left between the cotton and woollen materials, which sometimes remain open, and are sometimes sewed to. The pattern on the yellow ground is carried out with great freedom and irregularity. To the lower end is woven a fringed band.

4. Ornamented corner piece also with broad fringed band. In its general disposition and distribution of colours the design resembles that of Fig. 2. The serrated and dovetailed coloured strips cross the warp at an angle of about 30°. Yellow and violet brown figures are shown in the blue and yellow strips respectively, running in double rows and with their heads facing each other. A careful study reveals an animal head in profile, to which is attached the body treated almost as an arabesque.

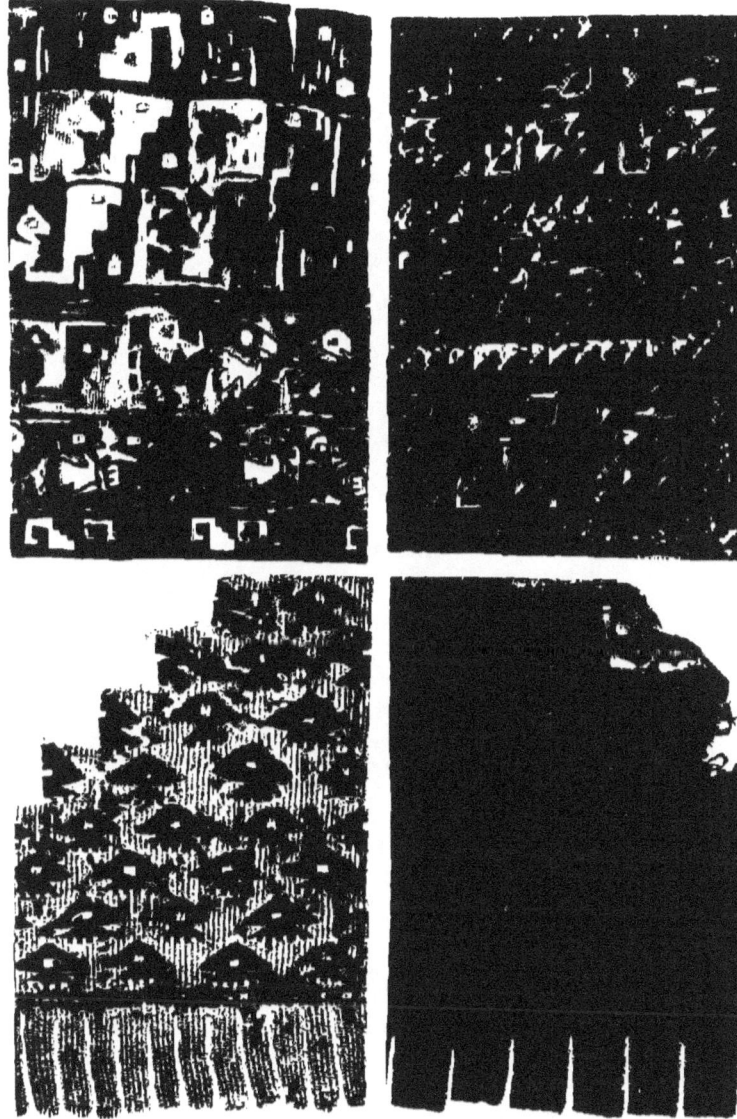

PLATE 64.

ORNAMENTED CORNERS.
(Natural size.)

Two Gobelins corners woven to cotton materials of one colour have already been figured on Plate 63, and further instances are here given in Figs. 1—3. In Fig. 4 the dress material is merely decorated with a few separate ornaments.

Fig. 1. Large Gobelins corner with bird motive. The hypothenuse of the triangle forming the corner is here indented with unusually large steps. Peculiar also is the framing of the ornamented spaces by four coloured stripes, which, although directly woven on, look like attached braiding, especially as in the coloured borders running parallel with the warp the slits occurring in the Gobelins weaving were drawn together by a fine stitch. The pattern shows three inclined coloured stripes, which are separated by narrow interlocked undulating bands. In the stripes is introduced in diverse dispositions of the colours a bird-figure with a huge head, disproportionately large eyes, hooked beak and claws, apparently a Condor, or rather his mate, the crest being absent. The lowest stripe shows two birds only; the central yellow stripe regularly traverses the entire ornamented corner, while the upper stripe is disposed by the steps of the hypothenuse into three separate parts each containing the figure of a Condor.

The whole design is less distinct than elsewhere, the several figures here entirely lacking the usual frame which, for instance in Fig. 2 is so very effective.

2. Wide Gobelins corner with animal motives. Two different animal figures are introduced in the coloured stripes which intersect the warp at an angle of 45°. The lowest stripe, of which a small corner only falls into the design, shows a solitary Condor decked with the characteristic crest. This motive is repeated five times in the third stripe which is also yellow. In the second red stripe between these two rows of Condors may be recognised a three and a half times repeated and strongly conventionalised form of a crestless Condor, whose body and wings are represented by a zig-zag figure. The upper edge of the corner is formed by the four steps of the topmost coloured stripe, by which the transition is effected to the one-coloured fabric. Each step contains the figure of the animal already represented on Plate 63a. With the exception of the yellow figures in the red stripes, the several animals are executed in diverse colours, while indentations and meandering bands are introduced between the broad coloured stripes. The lower edge of the corner is thickened or padded, as it were, by the ornamental hem being turned over.

3. Small closely woven Gobelins corner, whose hypothenuse is divided into seven steps. To each step corresponds a horizontal stripe of the red ground bordered by yellow lines, in which an animal motive in three colours is repeated several times. The design represents a conventional quadruped in the act of running, whose head is indicated by an eye, and whose long tail is turned up over his back. Each figure as well as the yellow lines between the several stripes is edged in black, while the steps of the hypothenuse are bordered both by a black and yellow stripe. The lower edge of the corner is finished off with yellow and black braiding. The Gobelins corner was sewed to the one-coloured fabric, the junction being effected by an over-stitch running parallel with the edges of the steps and worked in bright threads, which appear on both sides of the material as a raised braiding.

4. Corner of a loosely woven brown material, in which squares disposed in rows are interwoven with bright threads.

PLATE 64a.

COTTON CLOTHS WITH ORNAMENTAL CORNERS AND HEM.
Natural size.

The cotton cloths are decorated with bright edgings and borders quite in the same way as the dress materials (see Plates 65 and 65a). It is no longer possible to determine with certainty the uses of these mostly undyed fabrics which were sometimes of a close, sometimes of a loose, often even of an almost gauze-like texture. The large sheets, often from one to two meters square, may have served as coverings, or possibly even for enveloping the body, the smaller, especially those of closer texture, for wrapping and packing up objects to be preserved. Of the larger pieces the corners alone are usually ornamented, showing in pairs a somewhat varying pattern, or else the same pattern executed in different colours. One pair is mostly broader and more richly embellished than the other, the two diametrically opposed corners being always treated as forming one pair. In the small pieces similar ornamented edgings are displayed, not unfrequently connected with a border repeated on the two opposite sides; or still more commonly the borders without corners form the hem, in such a way as to close up the warp ends of the fabric above and below, leaving both intervening hems unornamented. The large cloths are made up of strips, whereas the small ones are woven in one piece. The corners and borderings are either executed in the Gobelins style (see Plates 63, Figs. 2, 3; 64. Figs. 1, 2, 3 and 69b, Fig. 7), or, as in these specimens, are made to resemble hand-embroidery.

Fig. 1. Ornamental edging of a large cotton cloth. In the closely woven fabric is introduced in yellow and black wool a meander-like pattern, by which the outer part of the corner is bordered in step-like gradings. By the interwoven red wool, of an almost silken sheen, this triangular piece appears disposed in diamond-shaped fields enclosing a strongly conventionalised bird. The cloth, the corners of which were alone found well preserved, seems to have been about 2 meters long by 1½ broad.

2. Border of a small cotton cloth. On a narrow strip interwoven with bright wool stand animal figures separated from each other by three bright vertical lines, while on its inner side the border is edged by a narrow horizontal line. In the design all the figures are alike, representing that so frequently recurring animal, which here and on the following border (Fig. 3 and Pl. 64b, Fig. 2) appears in a somewhat modified form. The colouring is also varied in such a way that five consecutive figures are always of the same colour, as for instance red, as the intervening lines, while the next series is of some other colour, such as the blue of this specimen. In such changes no attention was at all paid to uniformity, deviations and irregularities in the colours being of frequent occurrence.

3. Ornamented corner and border of a small cotton cloth. Here border and corner are exceptionally carried out in uniform pattern, bright interwoven woollen stripes forming the support for rows of the animal with which the previous figure has made us familiar. Two of such rows run as a border along the hem, while above them are four others continually decreasing upwards, and serving to ornament the corner. The several animal figures are uniformly executed in two colours, the lower portion being mostly dark, the upper lighter or more vivid. Although the colours vary in the different stripes, all the figures of each row are invariably executed in the same way.

PLATE 64b.

ORNAMENTAL HEMS OF SMALL COTTON CLOTHS.

(Natural size.)

The hems of the small cotton stuffs are ornamented in diverse and often original ways. To the specimens figured on the foregoing Plate may be added the series here reproduced. Many pieces end simply in a coloured woollen border, while in others animal forms are woven in dark wool into the bright ground of the cotton material itself. The gay borders themselves are directly woven on, several of the fine warp-threads being twisted together in so many stout warp skeins.

Fig. 1. Near the warp end, terminating in small fringes, is a row of animal figures on a narrow border formed by two black woollen stripes. The motive is a stag, as unmistakably shown by the large antler. Such slight deviations as occur in the design of individual figures are easily explained by the unsteady or capricious character of free-hand work.

2. A rather broad bright woollen border forms the ground for figures designed in black of the so frequently recurring dog-like animal, here, as in Plate 64 a, Fig. 2, separated from each other by double vertical stripes.

3. Highly conventionalised animal figures, almost reduced to a mere ornament, stand in a compact row on a narrow yellow border, along the centre of which runs an elegant design executed in black.

4. The central portion of the border worked in black is occupied by a row of bird figures perching, or perhaps swimming, and separated from each other by spiral ornaments. The execution differs from that of the previous pieces, animal and ornament here appearing, now in black design, now reserved in white on a black ground. The continuous fields of the pattern thus form, as it were, the right and left sides of one and the same fabric.

5. Wide bird border, executed as in Fig. 4; on either side edged with red and yellow woollen stripes. Instead of forming the hem, as is so often the case, the border is inserted above it.

6. The hem of this loosely woven cotton cloth is formed by a broad woollen border of bright design and edged with a braid-like pad closing up the warp hem. Terminating the woollen border and woven with black wool to the material are bird forms disposed in twos back to back, thus forming double bird-figures.

7. Fringed cotton border to a loosely woven cloth. It agrees only in its style of ornamentation with the foregoing borders, for the frequently recurring animal, so peculiarly conventionalised that it can with difficulty be identified, is here worked in the Gobelins manner.

PLATE 65.

WOOLLEN TRIMMINGS OF COTTON GARMENTS.

(Fig. 1 — ⅓ of Fig. 2 — ⅓ Fig. 3 — ⅓ of the natural size.)

The transition from the artistically woven Gobelins robes to the simple unadorned dress materials of Plates 36 and 38 is effected by garments, in which a fabric of one colour is embellished with richly ornamented corners and borders. A few only have been found in good condition, the more strongly woven portions (usually ornamented in wool) having alone escaped destruction.

Fig. 1. A Gobelins border and corner of a garment, whose essential portion consists of a thick one-coloured cotton fabric, woven with great uniformity. The woollen trimming is so woven on that the common warp runs right through to the extremities of the fringe. The hem is formed by a broad border furnished with a yellow fringe, whereas the corner-piece terminates in narrow coloured stripes obliquely disposed. The ornament of the border consists of a row of conventional human figures, all of uniform pattern but diversely coloured. The large head is decked with a cap hanging down on both sides (Plates 45, 47, 53). The armless trunk rests on legs turned outwards and terminating in peculiarly arranged three-toed feet. The yellow border is edged above and below with the red bands traversed by a string of black pearls enframed in yellow.

The ornament of the corner-piece is formed by one of those interlaced patterns in which the ground and design are of like form. The small triangles disposed in oblique rows must apparently be regarded as birds' heads completely conventionalised to mere ornaments. This piece is connected with the garment itself in the same way as in Fig. 3, Plate 63.

2. Fragment of a cotton garment with woollen corner. The corner, worked in the Gobelins manner, is woven on to the dress as in Fig. 1. But here we miss the border edging the hem. The corner pattern consists of horizontal stripes into which are introduced indented rhombic figures with a green cross in the centre. Each of the six upper stripes contains a complete row of these figures, while two such rows occupy the lowest which is nearly twice the width of the others. Two narrow three-stranded woollen braids are sewed on the cotton fabric at some distance from the corner, with which they harmonise in colour and design.

3. Ruddy brown cotton fabric with inserted woollen border. To the cotton strip, which in the illustration is turned downwards, the border worked in the Gobelins style is directly woven. But its upper hem is attached to another piece of the same material by a coarsely-stitched seam. The pattern consists essentially of a human figure ending off in meandering lines. All are alternately reversed and united in a common band by means of diagonal step-like lines. Conventional birds with their triangular contour suitably fill up the intervening spaces.

PLATE 65a.

COTTON MATERIALS WITH WOOLLEN TRIMMINGS.
PORTIONS OF GARMENTS.
(¼ of the natural size.)

Fig. 1. To the brown cotton fabric is woven a broad brightly ornamented woollen border executed in the Gobelins style. The corner, which is strengthened and embellished in a similar way, presents the already frequently described step-like edging towards the garment, bird-figures being disposed in rows on the red ground. In the middle piece of the border, which is also red, is repeated in a long row the figure of that four-footed animal, which occurs so frequently and so diversely executed as an ornamental motive (Plates 53a, 64a, 64b, 66, 73, 93), and which may perhaps be identified as a dog. The several figures of the row harmonize exactly in design, while deviating from each other in colour. Like the birds in the corner, these animal figures are also outlined now in light, now in dark. The middle piece of the border is edged above and below with alternate narrow stripes, whose pattern might at first sight possibly seem strange. But a comparison with the corresponding edging in Fig. 2 reveals the peculiar meander, the skilful and varied application of which has produced so many characteristic ornaments of the old Peruvian industry. — The garment ends below in yellow tabs.

2. The dress, from which this piece has been taken, consisted of a brown cotton material with woollen border woven on. But it is distinguished from the other garments of this class by being composed of a number of narrow strips, and not consisting, like them, of one large piece. This deviation is conditioned by the insertion of narrow Gobelins stripes running in the cotton fabric vertically down to the border. To avoid the tedious labour of weaving in these Gobelins stripes, each several section of the garment has in fact been separately prepared, and to each the corresponding section of the border has been woven on. The garment consists accordingly of wide cotton strips with woollen border woven on, and separated by narrow Gobelins stripes with their corresponding border pieces. Hence the border of the several sections not being executed in exactly the same way, there appear striking irregularities, as, for instance, on the left side of the illustration. In its general disposition the border corresponds to that described in Fig. 1, only instead of the canine animal, we have here a llama, the several parts of whose body are diversely coloured. In the narrow inserted stripes bird-figures are interwoven facing now to the right, now to the left. The border strips are adorned at the edge with small fringes concealing the stitches required for the insertions.

PLATE 66.

BROAD GOBELINS WOOLLEN BORDERINGS.

(Fig. 1 = ⅓; Figs. 2 and 3 = ½ of the material size.)

Besides the ornamental pieces directly woven to the garments, numerous borders and edgings were also independently woven, to serve as trimmings for ponchos and cloths, or else to be used as bindings or girdles. The two classes may be easily distinguished by the warp running obliquely to the length in the first, lengthwise in the second. Three such separately woven woollen borderings are here brought together.

Fig. 1. A broad, border-like piece composed of eight narrow borders, each complete in itself, the red ground alone being common to all. The central strip consists of a broad border with the same ornament repeated in a continuous row in various shades of yellow, and disposed obliquely. It is composed of two triangles treated as heads, one facing upwards, the other downwards, and blended in one figure by means of their neck-like prolongations interlocked at a sharp angle. The narrow decorations attached to the horizontal lines of the triangles may pass for the head-dress, while the small red square may be taken for the eye. The rhombic space between the slender interlocked necks is occupied with a yellow cross. The borders enclosing the broad strip above and below are so far symmetrically disposed, that on either side a central and somewhat broader line is introduced between the two narrow ones. But the ornamentation departs somewhat from this strict uniformity. The central portion of the side borders shows a somewhat detached S-shaped motive in yellow outline only. In the narrower stripes the same ornament, with one exception, is repeated in more compact and continuous rows. But here, instead of the outlines, the whole surface is alternately coloured green and yellow. The oft-mentioned exception occurs in the lowest of the three upper stripes, where we have a strongly conventionalised human figure instead of the coloured S lines. The eighth border, little more than a mere red band, is sewed to the upper edge.

2. Trimming for border, with red woollen fringe. The warp is crossed at a sharp angle by the striped pattern, all the stripes shewing the same design, but with varying disposition of the colours. This design consists of uniform interlocked figures, which may be taken either for indented triangles, or even for animal faces, as on Plate 53a.

3. Broad trimming with red woollen fringe. Here also the warp is intersected at a sharp angle by the striped pattern, the same design again recurring in all the stripes. This consists of rows of conventional bird figures, so disposed that they seem to be mounting the steps of the serrated stripe. The design is seen most distinctly on the black ground, although also easily recognised in the other stripes. It recurs with five different dispositions of the colours. The numerous slits necessitated by the method of weaving impart a peculiar light appearance to the border, as if the effect of these slits had been from the first taken into account in studying the general impression.

To the border is sewed a narrow band loosely stitched on with red thread. This band, which serves to connect the red fringe, is ornamented with a pretty waved pattern.

PLATE 66a.

BORDERS AND BORDER-LIKE FABRICS.

(⅓ of the natural size.)

Fig. 1. Gobelins border. On the red ground is executed a pattern in yellow, green and violet and edged in black consisting of interlocked congruent figures. Each is formed by two sets of parallel lines equal in length and at equal distances one from the other. The sets, which intersect at acute angles, are so dovetailed that the middle of the lines in one is touched by the lower extremities of the other, while the free ends finish off in animal heads. The design is carried out with somewhat broad strokes vandyked on one side. Both sets of lines in yellow stand out conspicuously, whereas the green and violet sets, which are worked in the reverse direction into the yellow, are only partly visible. The whole forms a flat ornament, of which the border shows only a small and consequently incomplete section. The same motive is repeated in richer and more elegant style on Plate 69. Fig. 5, where, owing to the rounded forms, it takes more the appearance of an interlocked hook ornament.

2. White fabric with interwoven variegated ornament. The pattern of the border-like strip consists of two pieces separated by a line half yellow half red. On either side of this central line narrow ornamental stripes run obliquely across the border, and are so disposed that they meet at an acute angle in the centre. In the coloured stripes an undulating line and a number of regularly distributed spots are reserved on the white ground. To the right the stripes are alternately red and black; to the left both divisions of the several stripes retain these two colours, while the stripes themselves are considerably wider. The woollen ornament is further edged on the right with a narrow red hem, but remains without any edging on the left.

3. Border, whose pattern consists of diversely coloured rectangles disposed lengthwise towards each other, and with a figure 8 inserted. In the red figure round specks of the ground colour are regularly distributed, while both curved ends are treated as animal heads.

4. Border-like portion of a larger piece. A row of black and yellow fields, serving as spaces for conventionalised birds, is edged above by an undulating band. Each separate part of the ornament is outlined in red, and a good effect of colour is obtained by the grouping of the red with black, light and dark yellow.

5. Fragment of a broad Gobelins border. On the red ground is interwoven a boldly drawn almost black ornament with yellow edging.

6. Gobelins border with large human faces. In the broad central portion a human face, distinctly recognised by the eyes, nose and mouth, is repeated in alternately reversed position. Above the forehead rises the head-dress in the form of a triangle with vandyked streaks as of lightning darting out in every direction. Right and left of the face is introduced the large ear ornament, while the two claw-like feet are attached on either side directly to the chin. The general effect of this ornament is all the more striking that each face with the corresponding portion of the border is differently coloured, while the several parts are sharply cut off from the surroundings by coloured contours.

PLATE 67.

BORDERINGS AND SLEEVE TRIMMINGS.

(Fig. 1 = ⅔; 2 = ½; 3—6 = ⅓ of the natural size.)

Fig. 1. Gobelins border, or sleeve-trimming for a robe of the Poncho type. The warp, running lengthwise, is crossed obliquely by the pattern, which consists of conventional bird-figures, projecting hook-fashion from vandyked bands, and so disposed that every two rows interlocking occupy the whole space in the stripes (see Plate 39, Fig. 1). The ornament, executed in various colours, may also be regarded as a Meander running into bird-figures.

2. Gobelins border as a sleeve trimming. The design, carried out in two colours on a black ground, is composed of two parts, one of which, serving as a narrow edging, consists of vandyked triangles. In the broad main stripe there is woven a pattern of conventional bird-figures, like that of Fig. 1 but so large that it could only be partly executed.

3. Gobelins border with geometrical design. It is edged above by a padded binding, while to the lower edge are woven broad yellow tabs as a fringe. The pattern consists of blue and yellow crosses disposed in parallel zig-zag lines raised on a red ground. This design is all the more effective that a light transparent appearance is imparted to the whole by the numerous openings required in Gobelins weaving.

4. Gobelins sleeve-trimming with woollen fringe sewed on. A dull yellow forms the ground colour of the border, on which is raised a row of bright yellow squares. Each square contains an 8 shaped figure apparently formed by two conventional birds, joined together in such a way, that a common head and eye serves for the bodies turned in opposite directions. The bright yellow squares are surrounded by small, white bird figures disposed in regular rows. The narrow fringed edging is sewed on; nor does it altogether harmonise in colour with the ground of the border.

5. Red woollen border made up of three narrow strips. The surface of the upper strip is divided by a black meandering line into two nearly equal parts, which are differently coloured, and form two interlocked hooked ornaments. The stems, to which both hooked rows are attached, are broken by intruded wedge-shaped triangles, whereby the band-like appearance of the red and white coloured stripes is mainly produced. To this ornamental border is sewed a narrow red strip serving to connect a similar but broader strip uniformly broken.

6. Gobelins border with broad tabbed fringe. One of the most frequently recurring motives is reproduced on the border, which is edged by narrow lines in several colours. The yellow ground is intersected by oblique vandyked stripes, which are furnished with projecting hooks, executed in various colours, and clearly limited by a shaded contour. The whole is further so arranged that the yellow ground reproduces exactly the same design as the coloured stripes, although in reversed position. This altogether remarkable ornament consists of bird-figures completely corresponding with those of Fig. 1, except that the clearly indicated bird's heads of that specimen are here degraded to triangular figures. In fact the motive may in the simplest manner be reduced to a regular meandering line, parts of which have been changed by the addition of some unimportant indentations. This will be best seen by following the red outlines of Fig. 1 and tracing a sketch of the contour. The border served as a trimming for a garment of the poncho type, to which it had been directly woven.

PLATE 67a.

BORDERINGS OF GARMENTS.
Natural size.

The specimens of borders here figured vary greatly in quality, but they so far agree that all are woven on to the material to which they serve as trimmings.

Fig. 1. Richly ornamented woollen border with fringed appendage stitched on. Border and cotton dress have a common warp, two or more threads of the dress being united for the warp of the border. Thus is produced the rep-like texture, such as is here exhibited in the yellow and red edgings of the border. The pattern is singly woven, so that on the reverse the bright threads lie loosely together at considerable intervals. Anyhow this specimen must be classed with those, in which technique and bent of taste find advantageous expression. The design is not calculated merely for the narrow space of the border, but may be supposed continued in all directions. Although standing out most distinctly in the yellow lines, it still recurs in the other colours in a somewhat complimentary way, as has already been pointed out for several of the textile designs.

The motive consists of a bird, whose long neck is bent sharply back, while the body is conventionalised as a line furnished with three hooks, like Plate 68, Fig. 1. But the hooked line itself is also independently utilised as a motive for the sectional arrangement of the pattern. It forms long stripes converging at a sharp angle, and, as it were, giving rise to the bodies of the birds. A symmetrical ornament is similarly developed from the junction of every two pair of birds. Over the beaks of the birds united for this ornament and between their crossed bodies is introduced an arrow-head embellishment, but apparently only to fill up the space uniformly. The fringed edging is sewed on.

2. Cotton fabric so interwoven with black wool as to leave a portion of the material visible between the design. This is formed of diagonally disposed square fields, into which a conventional large-headed bird is fitted exactly. In the surrounding edging is adopted the hook ornament approaching the wave-line type, with an alternating change answering to the broken stripes.

3. Woollen border, in which the rep-like texture is less obvious than in most others of this class. In the woven material many irregularities are visible, pointing either at a less skilful hand or less care in its preparation. The hook-shaped figures of the design stand, with alternating colours, in a row unconnected together, and have been turned out some larger than others. In the woven portion of the fringed border sewed on with brown thread, spun yarn of varying thickness has been used.

4. Bordering, whose design is woven partly of wool, partly of cotton. It is distinguished from all the others by its prevailing white colour, which is comparatively of rare occurrence in designs, and then only in a subordinate way. The white ground is of cotton, wool being used for the geometrical design, which agrees very closely with Fig. 6 of Plate 68, and which stands out raised on the plain cotton ground. In the woven edge of the fringed hem black has been exceptionally used with the yellow. Black is also the colour of the thread joining the fringed trimming to the white edge of the border.

PLATE 67b.

WOOLLEN BORDERS OF COTTON GARMENTS.

Figs. 1, 2 = ½; Fig. 4 = ¼ of the actual size.

Fig. 1. Wide border ending in tabs, whose warp consists of the warp-threads of the cotton material united in strands. In the uniform design, executed in yellow and red, and disposed in sections, red lines form an edging to horizontal S-shaped figures, whose ends enclose animal faces. The rest of the space is occupied by red zig-zag lines, and the monotony of the yellow surfaces is relieved by the red spots reserved in them. The border is woven, not in the Gobelins manner, but with threads carried through. In the stripes edging the design above and below the black lines show effectively on the yellow.

2. Cotton fabric with Gobelins woollen border woven on. The strip is disposed by blue zig-zag lines in alternately blue and yellow trapeze-shaped fields. In each field a conventional human figure, woven in with red wool, follows the sides of the trapeze with its step-like outlines. Suggestive of eyes are the little squares introduced into each of the alternately reversed red figures. The spaces in the corners of the trapeze are filled with small ornaments.

3. Gobelins border woven to a loose cotton material striped in brown. On the red ground are woven at uniform distances and in alternating colours, figures so strongly conventionalised as to render it doubtful whether a human or bird motive was originally intended. The large bird-like heads furnished with an eye bordered round nearly coincide in all the figures, whereas the presumable body, in an upright position, is so arbitrarily treated that none of the figures quite agree. Prongs or teeth of varying length branch off from the shafts which form the bodies, and which are provided with a broad foot. The green and violet figures lack the black edging, and the whole series of figures is bordered above and below by yellow and black lines.

4. Ornamental edging of a cotton garment of a bright brick-red colour. It consists of a border with wide tabs and notched triangles projecting into the fabric. The triangles, connected by their warp with the cotton material, show smaller indentations than other stuffs of this kind (see Pl. 35, Figs. 2 and 4: Pl. 65a, Fig. 1). In the red triangular spaces are scattered small yellow, white, blue and black animal figures, consisting of a head and body terminating in a hook with arms or legs stretched forward. The triangles are separated from the tabs by a blue and red complimentary wave ornament edged with pale red and black lines. The tabs are in two colours, so arranged that the red ground of the border occupies half the space in each, leaving only to the lower half the usual yellow colour. In the red portion of each tab recur the animal figures of the triangles in a slightly modified form, and, as in the triangles, they are here also reversed, head downwards.

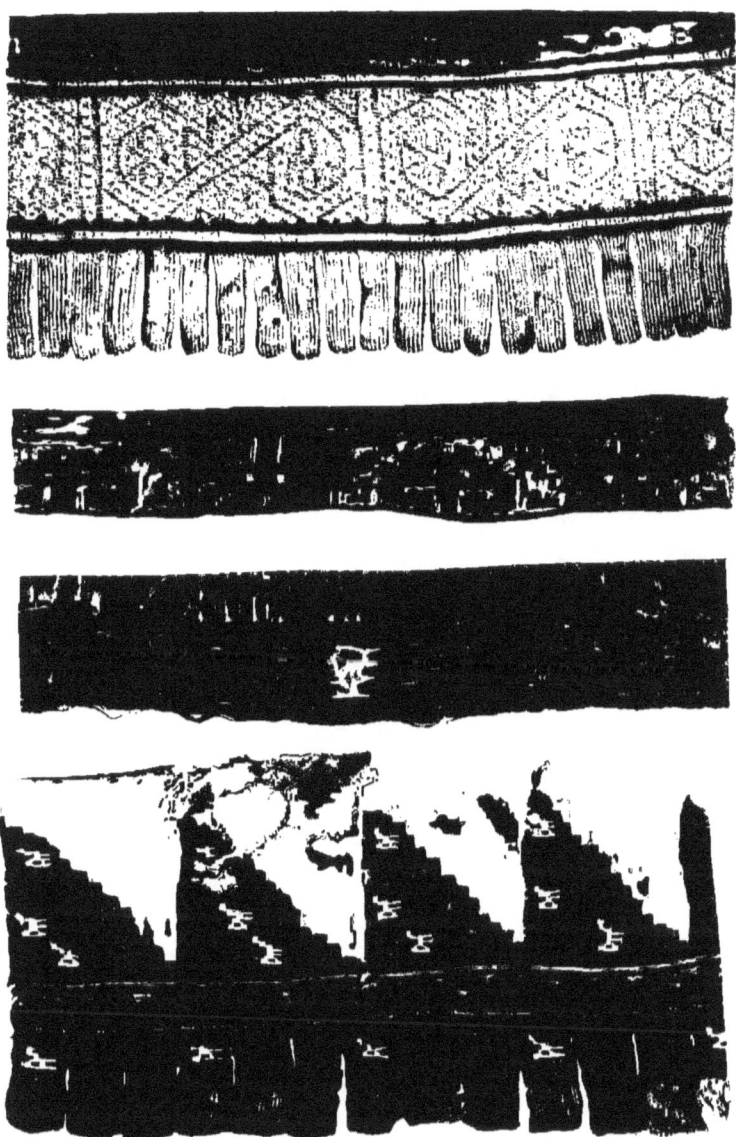

PLATE 68.

(Natural size.)

WOOLLEN DRESS BORDERINGS.

The six borders here figured were originally woven on to dress materials, as is evident from the oblique run of the warp. The specimens 1, 3, 4, 5, all complete within themselves, were in fact found with portions of the garments. Fig. 2 is executed in the Gobelins style; the rest are samples of real weaving, in which the many-coloured designs are loosely woven, as compared with the one-coloured bordering stripes. On the reverse side the pattern can scarcely be detected. Here the threads fall freely over large spaces, forming broad patches of colour in loose juxtaposition.

Fig. 1. Band-like border striped in brown and white. The middle and comparatively narrow portion is embellished with bird-motives so grouped in pairs as to form the elements of a figure. One of the birds stands erect, the other being reversed, while the long bill common to both serves as the connecting link. The way in which the neck seems curved back over the body corresponds to the attitude assumed in flight by pelicans and other long-necked birds. The body and wings are merely suggested by oblique stripes vandyked below. These figures in white on a brown ground alternate with others, in which the birds appear as brown on a white ground, the serrated wings of one colour thus fitting exactly into those of the other.

2. Gobelins border with geometrical pattern. On the red ground is a row of spiral yellow lines not otherwise connected together. The spirals are flattened at the sides, and, as required by the style of weaving, composed of serrated and straight lines. The space between the spirals is filled in with diversely coloured indented lines.

3. Narrow border with bird design. The frequently recurring motive of birds of this type ascending in rows an obliquely disposed stem is calculated for the embellishment of large surfaces. But when transferred to the narrow limits of a border it produces the impression of an arbitrary excision. The birds, drawn as large as the width of the border would allow, turn their heads backwards, and stand on a vandyked stripe of like colour, the grouping of the colours changing with the various stripes. The border itself is attached by a seam to a brown cotton fabric.

4. A somewhat wider border with bird design. With a few modifications the decoration of the central portion enclosed between many-coloured bands is the same as in Fig. 3. The stripes are more inclined; the bird-figures are smaller and look forward, and instead of being vandyked the stem supporting them is bordered by waving lines.

5. Woollen border with animal heads. The central portion of the border is divided lengthwise in diverse-coloured rectangles, each containing a much indented figure woven in a darker shade. Within this figure an animal figure (Plate 53a) is reserved, with pointed ears, and eyes and mouth suggested by coloured rhombs. In the central portion of the border all the colours, except the animal heads, are dotted over with black specks disposed in regular rows.

6. Border with diamond patterns. These designs, disposed in diagonal rows of uniform colour, stand out boldly from the closely woven yellow ground. As in Fig. 5 each diamond is occupied by an indented ornament, within which is again introduced a small rhombus encircled by regularly disposed black spots. Each part of the design is also outlined in black, and the whole arrangement recalls the patterns common in wicker-work. This border differs from all the others in the absence of any side edging formed by long coloured stripes.

PLATE 68a.

BORDER-LIKE WOOLLEN FABRICS.

(Natural size.)

It is no longer possible to determine with certainty the use of a number of border-like woven strips, which were obtained only in small pieces from much decayed mummy-packs. They may have either served as trimmings for larger garments, or formed portions of garments composed, as was often the case, of numerous narrow strips woven separately.

Fig. 1. Strips of a Gobelins fabric. The cotton warp runs lengthwise, the coloured weft consisting of woollen yarn. The strip is disposed in the direction of its length in a series of rectangles, each enclosed in several coloured stripes. In the alternately yellow and black but always uniform ground of the inner space a human face is introduced, encircled by a symmetrically radiating scalloped ornament. The long Gobelins slits have greatly expanded with the straining of the fabric.

2. Meander strip. A large Meander, partly running in step lines and filling the whole width of the material, forms the ground of the ornamentation, which produces a peculiar effect through the diverse colouring of the several parts, as well as through the design woven into the ground. For rhomboidal figures are here designed in dark brown wool, which appear scarcely affected by the various colouring, and adapted only to the disposition of the space. In the narrow arms of the meander, itself distributed in two coloured surfaces, these rhombs are grouped in notched rods. In the broad spaces at the convergence they become larger, here changed by a few added strokes and dots to human faces. — Apparently piece of a border.

3. Diagonally striped border-like fabric. Bright stripes run obliquely to the warp. The vandyked edges are enclosed in red, and in each stripe a meander line is worked in red thread, which in combination with red dots appears transformed to an ornament consisting of animal heads dovetailed together. The warp is of cotton, as shown by the slightly frayed lower end.

4. Narrow woollen fabric, showing in a superimposed row frequently repeated salamander-like figures, which appear as if seen from the under side. Between these quadrupeds are very imperfectly drawn animal figures facing each other in couples. All the figures are enclosed in black, and executed in yellow, blue-gray or green alternately. These figures are woven in by means of an underlying many-coloured weft, whose threads are inserted at both sides of the material, and appear on the upper surface only in the lines and spaces of the design, where they are joined in twos and worked into the tissue. On the reverse the threads lie loose, the fabric thus acquiring a double thickness, without gaining in strength.

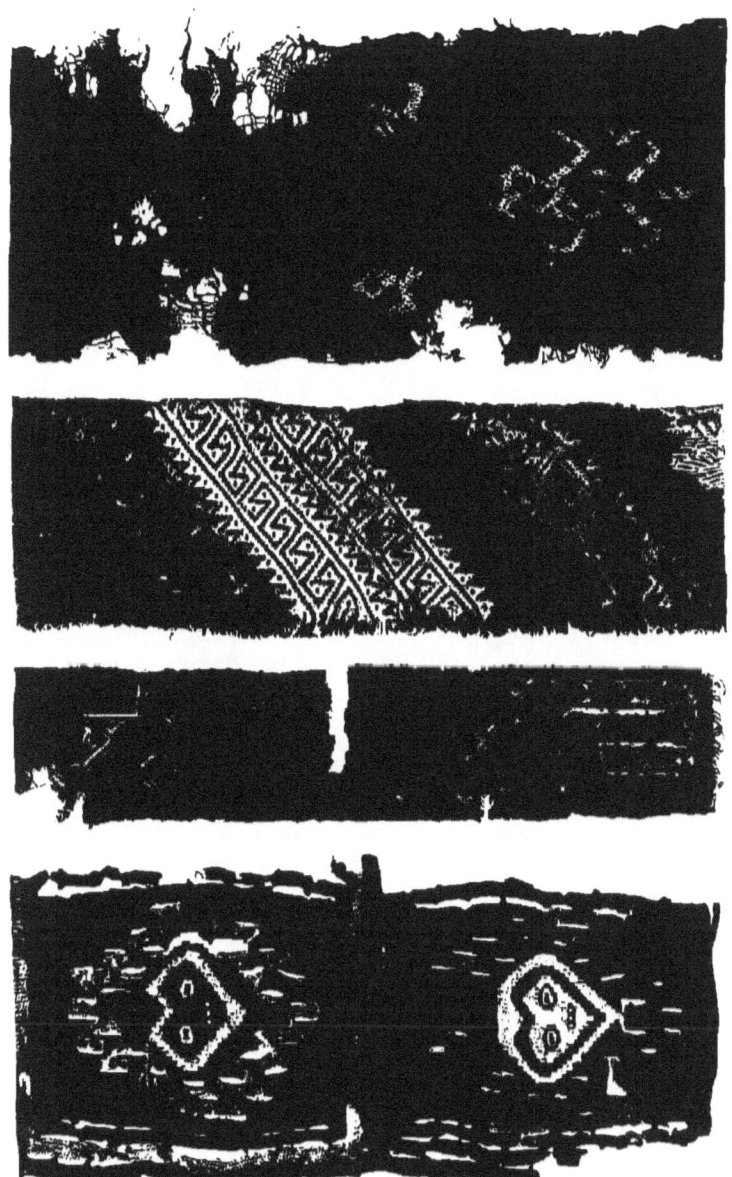

PLATE 68b.

WOOLLEN BORDERS AND COTTON DRESS MATERIALS.
(Fig. 1 — 3 = ⅓; Fig. 4 — 5 = ⅓ of the natural size.)

The five pieces here grouped together served as borders to decorate coarse cotton stuffs, to which they were directly woven. In their pattern they show the common peculiarity, that both the red ground and the figures designed on it are uniformly crossed by regularly disposed rows of black dots. The figures are enframed in black or at least dark lines. As regards the style of weaving they belong to the class of materials, in which the design is produced by the interchange of diverse colours in the woof, and often further modified by interweaving the woof-threads not singly but twisted two together.

Fig. 1. Figures executed in blue and yellow, representing an entanglement of broken lines, are repeated at regular intervals, the ends terminating in animal heads, as in Pl. 57, Fig. 2.

2. Double-striped border, the similarity of the stripes giving it the appearance of being composed of two pieces. The figures, as in Pl. 64b, Fig. 7, are so arranged that they seem on either side to run along the blue and black ornamental middle stripe.

3. The animal forms here represented in diverse colours but at like intervals betray a departure from the conventional style usual in woven materials (Pl. 53a; 64; 64 a and b; 65a). The form approaches that characteristic of earthenware (Pl. 93, Fig. 8; Pl. 100, Fig. 1).

4. Wide border distinguished by its rich design and delicate weaving. The ornament, developed in a square, recurs at short intervals along the whole length of the strip, varying however in the colouring of the several parts. It consists of a regular hexagon, in the present case executed in dark blue, with distorted human faces introduced in the right and left angles. Conventional human heads with large head-dress appear also in the centre of the upper and under sides, while from the four intervening angles are developed bands terminating in animal heads, as in Fig. 1, only here the red ground also reveals the form of a reserved animal face. The so far described portion of the pattern recalls the ornaments woven to the woollen ponchos (Pl. 75, Fig. 5, 8, 9). Within the dark blue hexagon one of those figures (Pl. 53a, Fig. 1) is reserved, that are so commonly used in wickerwork. The red space is also enlivened by an embellishment executed in yellow. The whole is enclosed in a square yellow frame, whose sides merge inwardly in alternate zigzag and waving lines.

5. Border disposed in longitudinal stripes. The warp is formed by the warp-threads of the associated coarse cotton material, each two being united in a single twist. A rep-like texture appears, however, only in the narrow parallel stripes, which are seen inserted between the broader, ornamental and doubly thickened stripes of the border. The ornamental stripes themselves are produced by the above-mentioned twists becoming again separated into their several strands, and then alternately utilised as two warp-threads for an upper and an under tissue. The introduced weft of the upper is red and black, of the under now yellow now green. Both tissues lie loosely on each other, except where the design of the pattern is effected by the interchange of both wefts. In each of these the threads are always taken in twos, whereby the breadth of the several coloured spots is conditioned. As shown by the reverse, the weft of the under tissue does not run through the whole length, hence can only have been introduced by the hand piecemeal.

PLATE 69.

WOOLLEN BORDERS.

(Fig. 1 - ; Fig. 2 = ¹; Figs. 3—6 = ¹/₃ of the natural size.)

Fig. 1. Gobelins border with tabbed fringe. By the narrow stripes of an elegant wave ornament the border is disposed in rectangles vertically superimposed, each showing a human figure on a red ground. In the figure of the upper field (front view) the small trunk supports a large head with ear-plugs standing well out, and decked with a top-knot raised above the hat-like covering and expanding on both sides. Below the out-spread skirt the crooked legs protrude with peculiarly applied large feet while the long arms terminate with large hands, each holding a rod-like object. In the lower figure, given in profile, the head is decked with a single stripe curved backwards. The upper part of the body is lengthened, the lower draped with a garment from which project stripe-like continuations. The bent legs are drawn in profile, but the feet and arms attached as in the upper figure. In the hands are two objects, whose nature can scarcely be surmised.

2. Green Gobelins border with yellow pattern. In the upper and lower figures unmistakable is the large face with its two outstanding ears and side headgear or antlers. The lower portion of both is formed by the conventional body of a recumbent animal, whose curly tail may be indicated by the small square attached behind. From the head one might suppose a human figure had been intended; but the lower portion must apparently be taken for the body of an animal. Between these two a similar but far more conventionalised figure is introduced in reverse attitude.

3. Red Gobelins border with human figures. Square black enclosures divide the ground into distinct fields separated by narrow intervals, and each containing the same human figure. In the broad face one eye is black, the other white. To the head-dress are attached peculiar ornaments, while large ear-plugs are applied to the sides of the face. Legs of peculiar shape are fitted to the scarcely suggested body, while the arms are represented by broad yellow cross stripes.

4. Woollen border with bird pattern. Here the yellow design on red ground runs in oblique stripes across the breadth of the border. Each stripe is edged on one side by a straight, on the other by an indented line. On the straight line are raised birds' heads surrounded by a reserved hooked pattern of the red ground. We seem to detect the form of a ray, within which the yellow bird head has been traced. The red ground is broken by yellow, the yellow by red dots.

5. Gobelins border with animal motive. The ornament already figured on Plate 66b, Fig. 1 is here reproduced, carefully and elegantly drawn, and coloured with great taste.

6. Gobelins border with human figures and geometrically ornamented hem. The central band-like division is encircled by a narrow hem adorned with geometrical figures. The pattern of the central stripe is formed by diversely coloured and peculiarly distorted human figures with spiral head-dress, large ear ornaments and three legs fitted directly to the chin. These legs are overlapped right and left by the dress, or possibly the arms, while an unusual expression is imparted to the features by the way the corners of the mouth are drawn down. For the sake of clearness the illustration is reproduced in brighter colours than the original, which is much decayed.

PLATE 69a.

PIECES OF INSERTION AND WOOLLEN BAND.

(Fig. 1 and 4 = 1/1; Fig. 2 = 1/1; Fig. 3 = 1/2 of the natural size.)

The fabrics reproduced in Figs. 1—3, and which were found in loose pieces, may have served as insertions of garments, as in Fig. 1, Pl. 60a. They present a striking contrast to other woven materials of similar style in their ornamentation and colouring, especially as regards the white ground peculiar to all three. In the ornamentation of the two first pieces the human form may still be recognised, which it is scarcely any longer possible to detect in Fig. 3.

Fig. 1. Rectangular piece of undyed white cotton, whose stout warp produces a rep-like tissue. A human form, clearly recognised by its head and face, is woven in the Gobelins manner on the white ground. The hat with the large attached head-dress and pendant continuations on both sides (Pl. 45, 46, 54), although only partly preserved, is still sufficiently characteristic in its execution. Both body and legs are represented by a reversed step-pyramid composed of coloured stripes and standing on a long red and black stripe. The arms and hands stretched upwards are also similarly formed.

2. The decoration, woven Gobelins-fashion to the white cotton stuff, is thus represented: — A system of cross stripes attached by an architrave by a peg indicated in blue and red bears at both ends a couple of superimposed and reversed pyramids or cones, on either side of which stands a human figure. The system of joists is executed in brown, the rest of the design enclosed in brown. The apex of each pyramid is light blue, while the base ends in uni-coloured stripes furnished with cruciform ornaments. The fabric has suffered so much from decay, that the human figures must be mainly conjectured from the large head-dress. To the strips of material narrowing downwards are sewed bright fringed borders.

3. Both sides of a somewhat lengthy woven material are edged by narrow borders ornamented with a scalloped meander executed in white and green. Its upper third section is occupied by simple coloured stripes, its lower by more richly ornamented stripes mostly coloured green, while the white cotton central section shows an ornament apparently also reducible to a human type: a large head wearing a certainly somewhat unusual head-dress, and a body suggested as a narrow trunk with four claws or toes attached to its lower end. Attachments projecting laterally from the trunk upwards may be regarded as arms, or as the detached ends of the girdle. Or else, and this suggestion is supported by the colouring, we have here the only instance hitherto discovered in Ancon of an attempt to apply floral ornamentation to woven materials. — The whole was executed in one piece after the Gobelins fashion.

4. Narrow band, in which the bright woollen thread is supported by a stout cotton warp. Peculiar is the frequent change both of colours and ornament, giving the whole the appearance of a piece of patch-work.

PLATE 69b.

SUNDRY PIECES OF WEAVING.

Pl. : 6 1/1. Fig. 7 4/1 of the natural size

Fig. 1. Narrow woollen band, disposed lengthwise in alternate red and white squares. Each of the red squares is embellished with a bird-figure, executed in the Gobelins manner, and all are enframed in black, but display differents arrangements of the colours. Some of the dyes must have been more injurious than others to the wool, exposing it to more rapid decay. Thus it happens that in several places, and especially in the birds' heads, the warp-threads alone of the texture have been preserved.

2. Wide border-like woollen tissue. Red and yellow woollen strips twisted together are united in a simple pattern, which is again divided by black zigzag lines running crosswise.

3. Gobelins border. The red ground is disposed by a brown framework into large squares filling the whole breadth, but which, instead of being directly joined to each other, are separated by narrow coloured stripes. All the squares are crossed by regular rows of cruciform figures edged in black. Six such rows occur in the width of the piece, every three in alternate blue and yellow colours. Cotton warp with woollen weft.

4. Narrow red Gobelins band with animal figures; divided by yellow stripes into rectangular fields. Each shows a front view of the so frequently recurring dog-like animal, executed however in different colours. All the coloured spaces are edged in black.

5. Soft woollen material. On the dark brown ground are interwoven yellow almost leaf-shaped figures disposed in regular rows.

6. A thick, strong rep; the grey brown ground crossed by dark zigzag stripes.

7. Cotton stuff of uniform colour with ornamental corner woven on (see Pl. 63—64b). This step-shaped corner is disposed in light and dark squares, in each of which is interwoven a double bird alternately light on dark, and dark on light ground.

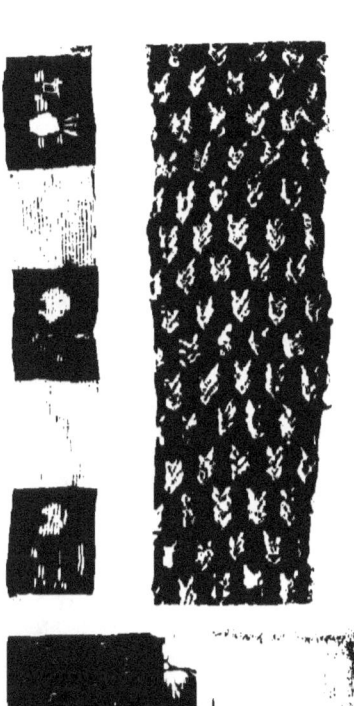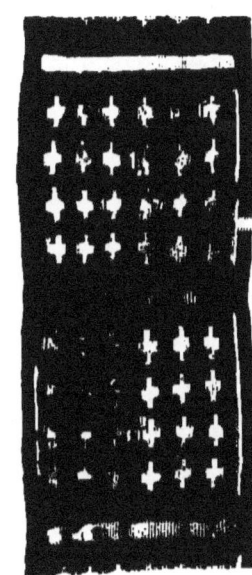

PLATE 69e.

DIVERSE KINDS OF SIMPLE DRESS MATERIALS.

(Natural size.)

Fig. 1. Stout woollen fabric of the most usual description. The warp consists of finer, the woof of stronger threads, whereby a reps texture is produced. As a finish off the warp ends are twisted together in fringes, in such a way that their loops, bent back and upwards, are secured and strung together by a last woof-thread afterwards passed through. The sides of the piece are strengthened and made firmer by hemming.

2. Coarse cotton stuff, in which warp and weft threads are of about equal strength. But the warp threads being unevenly spun and thicker in one place than another, this fabric also has at least partly acquired a reps-like appearance. Here the finish of the warp is effected by inserting strands, which fill up the lost space in the loops of the warp.

3. Brown and white checked cotton stuff.

4. Coloured striped cotton reps. In some of the stripes additional ornaments are produced, by allowing certain threads of the warp to lie loose at regular intervals.

5. Blue and white checked cotton stuff.

6. Coarse almost reps-like cotton stuff crossed by a figured stripe. In the warp of this stripe yellow woollen alternate with the cotton threads, while the design is effected by the woof passing, in regular recurrence, once or oftener now under one now under another of the warp-threads, without binding them. The design of the middle stripe nearly corresponds to the figure woven in the material, Plate 57, Fig. 2.

7. Piece of patchwork. Hundreds of small square bits of cloth, each woven separately, are stitched together in a single garment. The material here employed consists of very fine spun cotton. In the garment, of which a portion only was recovered, the blue, brown and white squares were disposed, according to their colours, in diagonal rows forming large geometrical figures.

8. Coarse woollen stuff with a single dark stripe bordered by two lighter stripes. Here also the finish of the warp effected by a thicker woof is distinctly perceptible.

PLATE 70.

LOOSELY WOVEN AND RETICULATED STUFFS.

Natural size ?

Fig. 1. A loose fabric of very unevenly spun white yarn; part of a piece 43 centimeters broad, probably prepared on the frame. The warp-threads lie closer than those of the weft. The yarn is so tightly twisted that, owing to the looseness of the texture, in many places the threads have curled up, thereby imparting great elasticity to the fabric.

2. Veil-like fabric of light blue yarn; perhaps afterwards dyed as a finished piece. As in Fig. 1 the curling of the fine unevenly spun threads produces a crape-like elasticity. The warp ends are twisted together as fringes, and their loops linked to the last weft-threads. Part of a larger piece.

3. Yellow woollen fabric. The threads crossing each other in a simple linen binding lie so far apart that the whole acquires a lattice-like appearance. Cloth like Pl. 43, Fig. 4.

4. Gauze-like reticulated cotton fabric disposed in squares by arranging the threads now closer now more loosely, at uniform distances in weft and warp. In this specimen occur two kinds of binding. The simple linen binding is shown in the systems with more closely disposed threads enframing, as it were, the squares. On the other hand the lattice work of the squares is produced by placing each weft-thread in the looping of every two warp-threads. At the same time this looping prevents the threads from shifting, which, as in Fig. 3, would be otherwise unavoidable.

5. Reticulated cotton fabric. This open textile, whose small meshes are grouped both in vertical and diagonal rows, is produced, as in the lattice work, Fig. 4, by an interlooping of the warp-threads by means of the weft, but in a different and more intricate series of rows. And here it will be noticed that the warp-threads consist of finer, the woof of stouter yarn.

6. Cotton cloth 95 centimeters wide. This textile is similarly prepared, only the binding is far looser than in the foregoing. All the fabrics in this and the following Plate were undoubtedly woven in frames, and intended for wrappers.

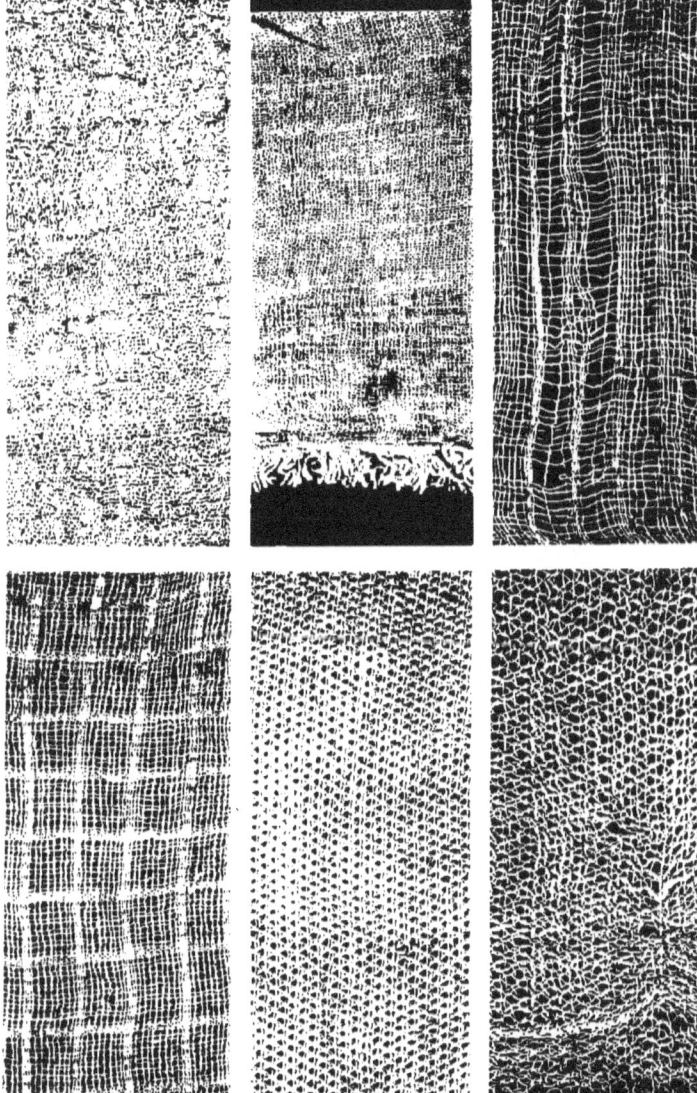

PLATE 70a.

LOOSELY WOVEN AND RETICULATED COTTON STUFFS.

(Natural size.)

Fig. 1. The Material corresponds in texture exactly to Fig. 4 of the previous Plate, the stripes and checks being effected, although on a larger scale, both by simple linen binding and by looping of the warp-threads. In this specimen the curling of the yarn is specially conspicuous.

2. Loosely woven textile with simple linen binding and reticulated pattern. This pattern is produced by the woof effecting a looping with the warp threads, not uniformly over the whole surface, but only in certain places, which here run in diagonal lines.

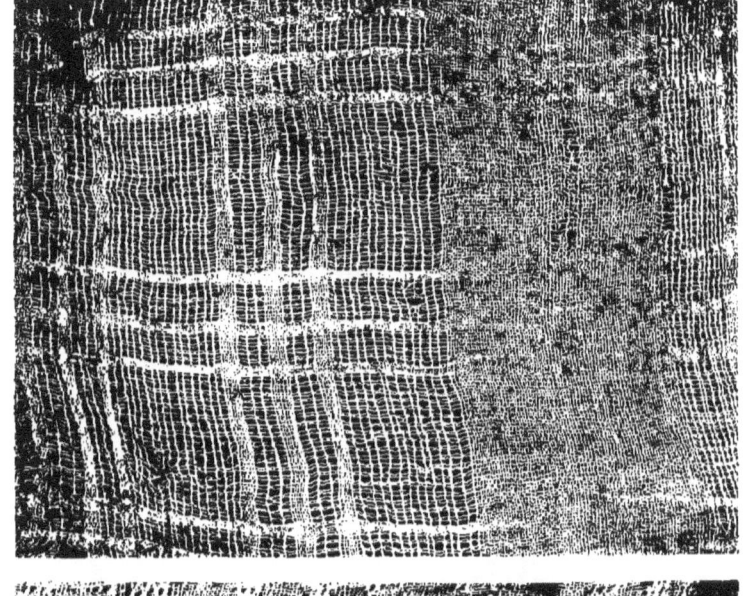

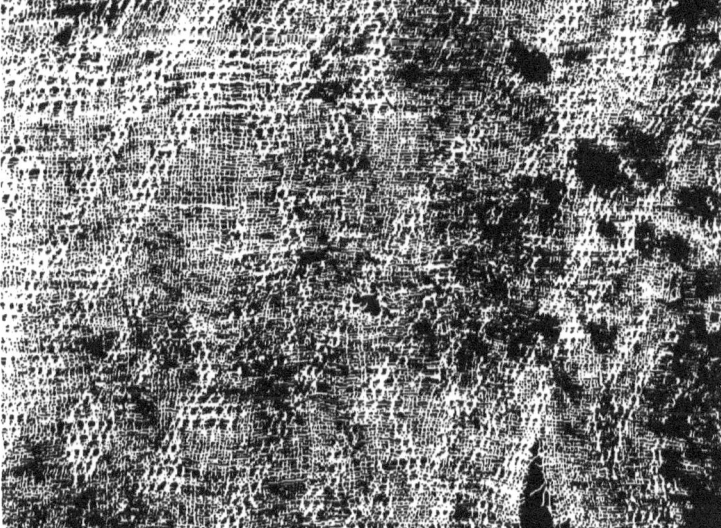

PLATE 71.

COTTON STUFFS RETICULATED AND ORNAMENTED WITH NEEDLEWORK.

(Fig. 1 — 5; Figs. 4—5 = ⅓ natural size.)

Fig. 1. Part of a very artistic cotton border, which probably formed the trimming of a robe perhaps of the talaris type. This piece, which is much damaged by mould, consists of two differently prepared parts, each woven separately: The border proper, 20 cm. broad; and a plain strip 11 cm. broad finishing off in narrow fringes not shown on the Plate. Both parts are brought abruptly edgewise together and joined by a scarcely perceptible seam, which begins at the left upper corner of the illustration 38 mm. below the intersecting line. The border itself is made up of 19 separate wide stripes, ten of which have a very thick reps-like, and nine a canvass-like texture. The warp-threads run lengthwise, consequently parallel with the stripes, and are so finely and closely woven that about forty go to a width of one centimeter. In order to weave the border the warp was strained with as many intervals as there were canvass-like stripes inserted. All the stripes of the thick tissue have a common woof, which at first lay freely open between them without any binding. But afterwards the loose lying woof strip was changed to a canvass work by drawing in the longitudinal threads. This process was so effected, that every two adjoining threads of the short woof continually cross each other round the longitudinal thread, whereby the latter is kept in its position in the way also shown on Pl. 70, Fig. 4. The ornaments displayed in the wide central and two of the side stripes are introduced into the canvass-like thread system by a kind embroidery, and the pattern of the central stripe corresponds almost exactly with that figured on Pl. 67a, Fig. 2. The surface is disposed in rhombs, whose alternate sides are occupied with meandering hooks, and each of these rhombs contains a conventional bird. The same bird motive also recurs in the two narrower stripes (see Pl. 104, Fig. 27—29). In the attached plain strip the warp runs right and left, not up and down, as in the border.

2. This stout cotton material shows openings disposed in rows, to produce which short stretches of the warp were left in weaving without any weft throughout the whole breadth. A thread afterwards passed through the loose warp-threads in the direction of the weft gathers each five of the warp-threads in a bundle by an interlacing process.

3. Tissue prepared as in Fig. 2; 26 cm. long, 12 broad.

4. and 5. The reticulated border is prepared by twisting together in groups the loosely lying warp-threads by means of threads which do not belong to the tissue, and which at the same time serve to connect the adjacent strands at the angles of their knee-like curvature.

In these specimens the reticulated work might seem to have been effected by drawing out the threads. But so far from this being the case, a closer inspection shows that in the weaving process the respective spaces were left free, in order afterwards to be further worked up by inserting fresh threads.

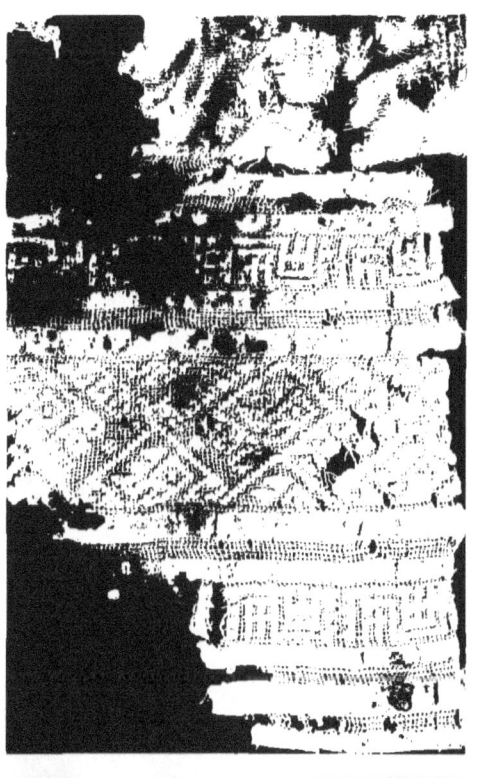

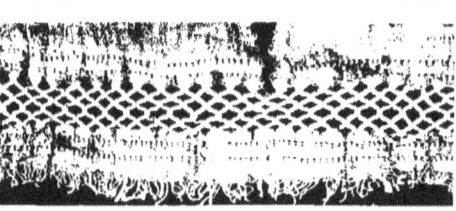
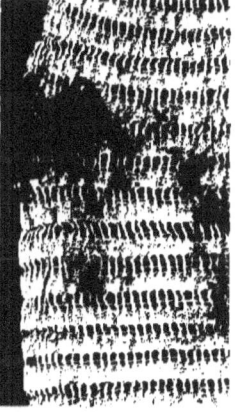

VII.

POUCHES.

(PLATES 72–74.)

Where no arrangements are made for holding and carrying various indispensable objects in the garments, pockets must be worn specially prepared for this purpose. Such was the case with the ancient Indians, as is shown both by the representations on the earthenware and by the large number of pouches found in the graves. The character of these pouches was modified according to the various uses for which they were intended. Finely worked woollen bags embellished with rich designs were worn suspended by stout bands from the shoulder, while simple cotton pockets served for ordinary use, to keep small articles in the house, or were partly prepared for the service of the dead, perhaps to represent the more valuable pouches. A pouch of peculiar type is figured on the first Plate of this section. Such girdle pouches served apparently to keep the Coca, as may also be inferred from the opening introduced especially in the smaller specimens in the middle of the long side.

The pouches generally display quite a peculiar style of ornamentation. In those made of wool highly intricate animal motives are used, while the cotton girdle pouches are frequently embellished by means of painting in a way nowhere else observed.

These girdle pouches, as well as the small fobs attached to them, contain nothing but dry leaves; but in the woollen hanging bags were found all kinds of implements, besides the scarcely ever absent stones for slings.

Plate 72 was prepared by Herr Schmidt, all the rest of this Part by Herr Paul Schulz.

PLATES OF PART VII.

94. Large and small girdle pouches	Plate	72
95. Woollen hanging bags	„	73
96. Woollen, Cotton and Net pouches	„	74
97. Pouch Materials	-	74a

PLATE 72.

LARGE AND SMALL GIRDLE POUCHES.

(¹⁄₃ of the natural size.)

To the Indian dress, consisting essentially of the short poncho and of loosely worn wraps, the suspended pouches for the reception of provisions and all sorts of useful little objects, must have formed an indispensable appendix, especially on journeys and hunting expeditions. Hence bags in the most varied forms and sizes, and in every variety of ornamentation and material, are the most frequently recurring of all objects deposited in the graves. To the suspended pouches two Plates (73 and 74) are reserved. Here are represented such wallets as were worn round the hips. Two of the smaller girdle-pouches are figured on Plate 74.

Most of the girdle-pouches seem to have served for carrying Coca. Some however were also found, which were stuffed with other leaves and stitched up all round. These must apparently have been intended exclusively for sepulchral purposes. Others, doubtless those required for daily use, have in the centre of one of their long sides a funnel-shaped attachment, which may have served for filling and emptying them.

Fig. 1. Large pouch sewed up all round and on the lower side embellished with a row of small bags. The thin cotton material would seem to have been painted before being formed into a pouch; for the painting extends to the front and reverse without regard to the effect of the design. The pieces at the side ends are squared in black and white, while the central portion shows a complexity of figures, among which may be recognised a frequently repeated worm-like animal and a small human form. The small fringed bags attached below are made of a cotton stuff specially woven for this purpose. Their front sides are more or less richly ornamented with bright wool. They are sewed up all round and stuffed with leaves.

2. Brown Coca-pouch. Ornamentation effected in a simple way with white lines. The attached little bags, alternately brown and blue, are similarly treated.

3. Large girdle-pouch, the painting, as in Fig. 1, extending over the whole surface. Both ends show stripes with wave-ornaments; the central portion another entanglement of figures, amongst which the worm-like animal is again conspicuous, but here with two heads, one at each extremity.

4. Small, carefully worked bag. The brown cotton material is embellished only on the front side, this being effected by white interwoven squares, with a seated animal reserved in the centre. In the body of each of these animals a bright spot is interwoven. Here the strings are unusually strong, each of the triple bands having been woven in one piece.

5. Gray pouch. The interwoven ornament is scarcely any longer perceptible, the coloured woollen threads having mouldered away. A few white outlines and some detached coloured spots have alone survived. To the middle of one of the long sides is attached one of the above-mentioned funnel-shaped bags, which by means of a string could be easily closed up.

6. Red pouch exactly like the foregoing. The meander pattern interwoven with white thread is partly decayed.

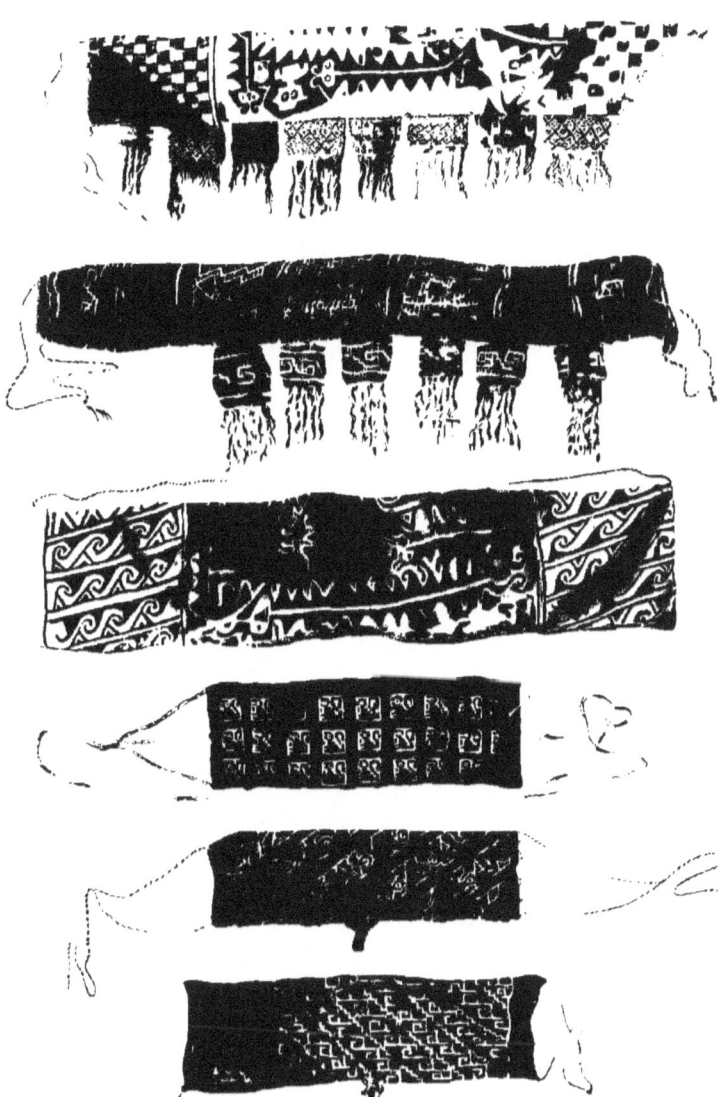

PLATE 73.

WOOLLEN HANGING BAGS.

(1/4 of the natural size.)

Amongst the hanging bags those made of wool are particularly distinguished by their careful execution and elegant ornamentation, often of quite a peculiar type. The finest and most highly embellished are made of fabrics expressly prepared for the purpose, as appears from the specially adapted pieces and patterns. Others have been sewed together of already existing scraps of cloth. The bags consist mostly of a single piece, although some occur made up of two pieces, or of narrow bands. Special care was bestowed on the sewing, the bright or many-coloured braid-like woollen stitches often contributing to the decoration of the bag. Strong, round, or else more or less wide, woollen bands, harmonising in colour and design with the bags, serve to suspend them. In a few cases only can such suspenders have been altogether absent, or replaced by simple strings. The mouth either remained quite open, or else was closed by drawing together a net pouch. Such appliances were in many instances attached directly to the edge of the bag.

Fig. 1. Bag of the commonest type, made of a woollen fabric sewed together on both sides.
2. Woollen bag, horizontally striped with elegant but simple patterns belongs, like Fig. 1, to the most frequently recurring forms.
3. Thick woollen bag with rich design, closed on three sides with a thick hem. The transition to the suspender is effected by wide many-coloured insertions.
4. Small, badly preserved woollen bag, with netted closing (Plate 74, Fig. 1).
5. Small Gobelins bag, design consisting of a peculiarly conventionalised human figure.
6. Small, yellow woollen bag, with stripes ornamented in black, in which two pair of highly conventional human figures are so interwoven, that the design appears alternately light on a dark, and dark on a light ground.
7. Large woollen bag, with round ornamental suspender. The adapted pattern repeats, with the same alternation of colours as in Fig. 6, a simple design like that of Plate 67, Fig. 2.
8. Oblong bag, with rich pattern of conventional animal forms, disposed in two stripes, once in yellow on a brown, and then in brown on a yellow ground.
9. Bag ornamented in the same style as Figs. 5 and 8. The pattern, worked with the breadth of the stripe, consists of highly articulated and strongly conventionalised human and animal figures. The mouth of the bag could be closed by introducing a band.
10. Small woollen bag with elegant, specially adapted pattern. Six bird-figures disposed in two rows, three light on a dark, three dark on a light ground, are bordered by narrow ornamental stripes. Bag provided with net closing.
11. Gobelins bag with net closing. Pattern formed by a meandering stripe transformed to bird-figures.
12. The bag, made of a woven fabric prepared for the purpose, displays as ornament a recumbent animal figure, whose tail again finishes in an animal head, surrounded by a not altogether symmetrical frame and small animal faces.
13. Small bag with a net closing and small diamond pattern.
14. Gobelins bag sewed together of three narrow strips.
15. Coarsely woven purse-shaped bag.

www.ingramcontent.com/pod-product-compliance
Lightning Source LLC
Chambersburg PA
CBHW032108220426
43664CB00008B/1182